Questioning Makes The Difference

by Nancy L. Johnson

Pieces of Learning

©1990 Pieces of Learning
www.piecesoflearning.com
CLC0072
ISBN 0-9623835-3-8
Printing No. 151413
Printed in the U.S.A.

To Joe Wayman

Who taught me everything I ever
wanted to know about questions—
except maybe what to do with the
answers!

QUESTIONS WITHOUT ANSWERS

What good are questions without answers, answers without questions?

The needle in my haystack is the needle that's in question.

It's never found the stitches, but it keeps it all together

Like my thoughts without the answers, QUESTIONS ARE ALL MINE.

What good is joy without the laughter, tears without the sorrow,

Pain without the hurting, time without tomorrow?

A maker of the peace who has to fight to get his way?

A fighter for the freedom, afraid of being free?

What good's a room without a window, a window without glass?

A song without the singing, a man without a past?

What good's a rhyme without the reason, time without the season?

Age without the beauty, youth without the wisdom?

A dancer without feet, a runner without races?

A race without an ending through a crowd that has no faces?

A suitcase standing empty, destination still unknown,

A journey that you travel if you never travel home?

What good are questions without answers, answers without questions?

The needle in my haystack is the needle that's in question.

It's never found the stitches but it keeps it all together

Like my thoughts without the answers, QUESTIONS ARE ALL MINE.

INTRODUCTION

This book is about questions and triangles. Actually, it is a book about combining questions and triangles. A triangle is a fascinating shape not quite a square, not quite a circle. Architects know that triangles are one of the most powerful forms the building industry uses. Their strength lies in the BALANCE between the three sides and three angles. Each side, each angle must be the same weight, same length, etc. or the balance is upset and the triangle collapses.

So it is with Questions. There are many DIFFERENT kinds of questions. Each is important. However in most classrooms teachers consistently ask basic knowledge level, right/wrong answer questions. This book attempts to teach the reader how to BALANCE basic recall with divergent questions. Specific techniques help teachers "partner" reproductive/productive questions, convergent/divergent questions, and low level/high level thinking questions. There are suggestions to make questioning an ACTIVE rather than passive activity. This book uses triangles to help the reader visualize this balancing and partnering process.

Every teacher is looking for that magic key to unlock the various learning doors that his/her students must open. Of course, there is no real magic, only hard work and perseverance. If there is a key, it is found in the teaching techniques that are carefully developed and refined by individual teachers. The question is: What is the teaching technique that is the most flexible and practical? The answer is: QUESTIONING! Teachers who are good questioners motivate their students, stimulate high level thinking, encourage creativity, and enhance self concept in their students and themselves. You just can't ask for more than that!

▼ WHO NEEDS THIS BOOK?

▲TEACHERS▲ THAT'S WHO! WHY?

Differentiated questioning doesn't add to the burdens in the classroom. Most teachers have enough to do. What questioning does is bring fun and excitement to learning. It pulls teachers out of the comfortable rut of asking the same questions over and over, thereby teaching the same year over and over. *Divergent questioning is a teaching tool* to be used at any time, at any grade level, with any curriculum.

▲ ADMINISTRATORS▲ THAT'S WHO! WHY?

Questioning gives principals an effective process to evaluate teachers. It is also a prescriptive tool that gives teachers specific, concrete suggestions to *improve the quality of instruction.* On a personal level, administrators can strengthen communication with staff and parents by sharpening their questioning skills.

▲ PARENTS▲ THAT'S WHO! WHY?

Parents MODELING divergent questioning for their children *strengthens self concept* and improves school achievement. Many of the life support skills, such as making good decisions, communicating effectively, and solving problems creatively begin with good questioning.

▲ CURRICULUM SPECIALISTS/WRITERS▲ THAT'S WHO! WHY?

There is an unkind but valid label that is batted around the sacred halls of education. It has to do with what is happening to strong, challenging curriculum. The term is "dummy down." Some of the "new" curriculum tries to cover more information without regard for in-depth exploration. Simply put, it's quantity not quality. Differentiated questioning will *stretch the curriculum* vertically so students have time to research and understand ideas.

▲ SPECIAL EDUCATION TEACHERS▲ THAT'S WHO! WHY?

Whether it is slowing down the learning process or speeding it up, *questioning makes the difference.* Remedial students benefit from questions that simplify while gifted students benefit from those that challenge complexity. Divergent questions allow for differentiated responses from students with special needs.

▲ KIDS▲ THAT'S WHO! WHY?

Questioning is a learning tool that improves a student's communication abilities and study skills. It does not require a change in learning style or a piece of fancy equipment. All it takes is another human being *modeling* the process and *practice.* Questioning is particularly useful during cooperative learning activities. Students learn to ask as well as answer divergent questions while participating in cooperative groups. This active rather than passive questioning results in a more positive attitude about self and school.

▲ **Differentiated Questioning skills**
are reflected in the following goals for students:

▶ To Use My Imagination For Thinking In Different Ways

▶ To Have Fun Learning

▶ To Express My Own Feelings And Views
By Sharing My Ideas With Others

▶ To Learn How To Think Harder And Better
By Disciplining My Mind

▶ To Learn To Work Independently And With Others

▶ To Think Of New Ways To Do Familiar Things

From a Good Resource
The Faces of Gifted
by Nancy Johnson
Pieces of Learning 1989

▼ TEXTBOOK DEPENDENCY:
▼ A TRADITIONAL CONSPIRACY

As an educator, I learned a long time ago that the path of least resistance in my classroom was the ever present, ever faithful TEXTBOOK! Whenever I broke away from this **traditional** time-honored teaching tool, waves of guilt usually followed. There always seemed to be plenty of *"fuel for the fire"* from parents and fellow educators in support of textbooks.

"Those books were good enough for me when I was in school —they're good enough now!"

"Just stick to the textbook, dearie, and you can't go wrong."

"Cut out all the frills — just buy the basic textbook for each child and a manual for the teacher."

And my favorite: *"We've tried all that creativity, finger painting, divergent questioning, touchy,*

feely nonsense — it's time to get back to the basics."

And the beat goes on and on and on and . . . the result is a **conspiracy.** Who's involved in the conspiracy? Teachers, parents, administrators, school board members—just about everyone who is involved in educating children. However, teachers seem to get blamed first when the conspiracy is exposed. Those of us who become **defectors** from the textbook conspiracy risk ridicule, ostracism, or even dismissal from our jobs. No wonder many give up the fight and return to the trenches armed with a new set of textbooks. Some educators spend their entire careers searching for the special, perfect textbook with all the magic answers. Yes, I'm a defector. No, I don't believe textbooks are all bad.

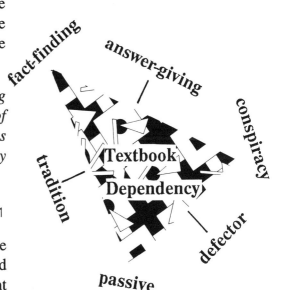

"When textbooks are used as PART of a curriculum, acting as organizational aids, discussion starters, or sources of factual information, they serve a purpose. But when used as a whole program, they encourage passivity and block inquiry because THEY TEACH ANSWERS, NOT QUESTIONS."

Vair, Independent School, 1981

I agree. Textbooks are predigested materials that force the learner into a **passive** absorption of information and a blind acceptance of someone else's opinion. As a teacher, a constant *"stick-to-the-textbook curriculum"* discourages MY initiative and frustrates MY creativity. Children who are taught by passive, **answer-giving, fact-finding** textbook teachers emulate that style in their own learning.

▲ QUESTIONING ETIQUETTE

Here is a sure-fire way to determine if you are **practicing** good questioning techniques. It takes a little courage, but the results are enlightening. Place a small tape recorder in your top desk drawer. If it has an external microphone, thread it out of the drawer to the top of your desk. Buy several 120 minute tapes and then record yourself teaching for one whole day.

I tried this and it worked well. Most of my students didn't know what I was doing. Every time I heard the recorder click I'd turn the tape over or stick in a new one. At the end of the day, I took the tapes home and in the privacy of my own home (behind closed doors) I listened to myself teach.

Between the laughter and the tears I began to evaluate my own questioning skills. For example, every time I asked a question that had a specific right or wrong answer, I gave myself a check. Every time I asked a divergent question, I gave myself an X. Then I simply added up my X's and my checks.

I was shocked to learn that most of the questions I asked were basic recall, right/wrong answer questions. I couldn't believe it! Before taping I thought I was a good questioner. I wonder how many divergent questions I would have counted if it had been a day when I didn't know I was being taped. Perish the thought!

I discovered two other questioning skills that were in need of improvement. I only waited about four seconds for a student to respond after I asked a question. And I answered about one third of the questions asked!

Here are a few suggestions about **when** to ask questions, **what** kind of questions to ask, and **how** to ask questions. I'll even throw in a few hints about what to do with the answers!

▲ DO'S

. . . *accept* all answers, even repeated ones

. . . make sure students *understand* what "open-ended" means

. . . ask questions when you are *really interested* in a student's thoughts

. . . ask questions after students have the *knowledge base* needed to handle the material

. . . place students in *partnering* or small group situations

. . . offer verbal and non-verbal *reinforcement*

. . . reward the *responding* not the response

. . . practice what you preach by *modeling* good questioning in your own life

. . . ask questions that motivate, and stimulate *emotion*

. . . sequence questions in terms of a student's *readiness* to learn

. . . ask questions that stimulate *evaluative* thinking

. . . ask questions that call for *guessing*

. . . ask questions that relate to a student's life *experience and interests*

. . . LISTEN TO THE ANSWERS!

. . . *vary* the technique of asking; take volunteers sometimes, call on students at other times

. . . allow sufficient *"wait time""* *after asking questions—most teachers wait less than 5 seconds*

. . . on occasion, *rephrase, clarify, or simplify* student responses

. . . *believe* in your own abilities and those of your students.

▼ DON'TS

. . . ask questions that fill time because you are not prepared for the lesson or activity

. . . follow the questions in the textbook word for word — be strong — use your own ideas

. . . isolate questioning skills and teach them as a separate curriculum

. . . ask only short-answer questions that result in one right answer

. . . ask questions just to find out what students DON'T know

. . . ridicule a student for an unusual, creative response

. . . ask questions that are embarrassing to the student

. . . limit your responses to "yes," "no," "great," "good"

. . . give up — good questioning takes practice

. . . be so serious — lighten up — have some fun

. . . ever say, "Wrong! Who knows the answer?"

. . . ANSWER YOUR OWN QUESTIONS!

. . . ask questions when you are very angry

. . . be judgmental.

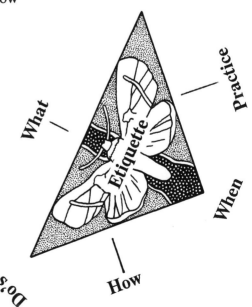

QUESTIONING MAKES THE DIFFERENCE

is part of a teaching process that is based on the following simple philosophy:

TEACHER: A CREATOR OF POSSIBILITIES

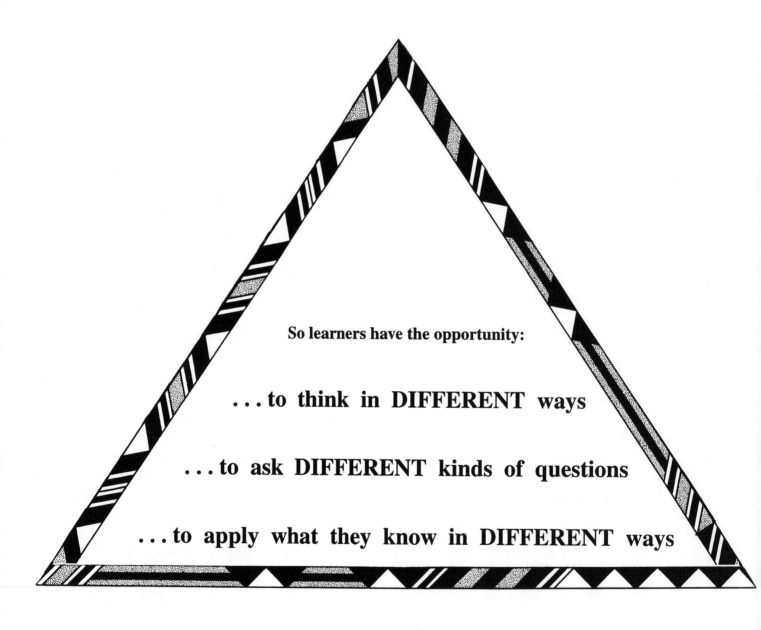

So learners have the opportunity:

. . . to think in DIFFERENT ways

. . . to ask DIFFERENT kinds of questions

. . . to apply what they know in DIFFERENT ways

▼ DO YOU TEACH FOR QUESTIONS OR

DO YOU TEACH FOR ANSWERS?

Why do teachers ask questions anyway? What is the real purpose? The objective? Is it to find out what a student doesn't know? Is it to catch the class clown off-guard? Is it to put that *"know it all"* gifted student in her proper place? Is it to make themselves appear smarter? Kids are born with an innate ability to see through adult hypocrisy. They are quick to sense an adult's true motivation. Never use questions to threaten, belittle, or accuse. Never use questions to cover a teacher's lack of knowledge or preparation.

Use questions to find out what students know. What they feel. What they need. Most important, use questions to stimulate and motivate MORE QUESTIONS! That happens if teachers start teaching for questions instead of answers.

QUESTIONING READINESS

The best curriculum, best preparation, and best intentions all are wasted if the students aren't **READY!** There are some teachers who are experts at Readiness. They're called primary teachers. They get kids ready to read, ready to write, ready to stand up, ready to sit down, ready to go to the bathroom, ready to line up, etc. etc. They are masters of the skill of Readiness. But think about it. They have to! They can't teach a little kid something if he isn't ready. If they do, they will find themselves re-teaching that skill — over and over and over! All teachers should follow the lead of primary teachers and spend more time preparing their students for learning. The results can be phenomenal.

So it goes with questioning and readiness. Extend the readiness process and learning is stimulated for longer periods of time. And the longer the learning/thinking process is kept alive, the more divergent and high level the responses. An important objective of the readiness process is TRUST. Trust between student and teacher establishes a powerful comfort level. The point is: Teachers, it's worth your time and effort to get students READY!

The divergent questioning process includes:

Quantity Questions   **Compare/Contrast Questions**

Feelings/Opinions/Personification Questions   **What Would Happen If Questions**

Quantity Questions serve as a readiness for the other three. The key to this particular kind of questioning is brainstorming. Proficiency in brainstorming lays the foundation for all other types of divergent questioning, so don't skimp on the Quantity Questions. All four kinds of differentiated questions attempt to change questioning from a passive to active mode. Have students ask divergent questions as well as answer them.

QUANTITY QUESTIONS

GOAL: To balance reproductive and productive questions

KEY: Brainstorming

Quantity questions are basically **listing** questions. However, most teachers ask only **reproductive** quantity questions. Teachers ask students to reproduce some knowledge or information they already know or should know. Consequently, those kinds of questions slight high level thinking and **creativity.**

The other kind of quantity questions are **productive.** The students **brainstorm** as many different ideas as possible — no right/no wrong answers. Teachers should ask both kinds of quantity questions, **balancing** the reproductive and productive thinking.

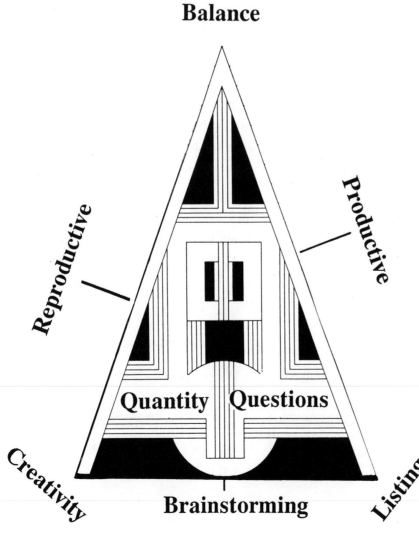

ACTIVE QUESTIONING

Students create their own lists of quantity questions. The teacher provides the answers (ideas) and the students supply the questions. In this case, the focus is on the questions, not the responses.

REPRODUCTIVE . . . . **PRODUCTIVE**

How many doors and windows are in this room?.................................

What are all the ways you can think of to get out of this room?

List all the materials in an upholstered chair...

List ways to use an upholstered chair other than as a piece of furniture.

What is 2+2, 3+1, 16-12?.................................

List ways you can think of to say "4."

Name the 50 states.................................

Imagine there are 4 states in the U.S. Draw the boundaries & name them.

List the time it takes you to walk, drive a car, or ride a bicycle to school.................

List all the ways you might travel to school.

How many colors are there in a rainbow? List them...

List all the feelings you get when you see a rainbow.

List occupations that require eyesight.....................

List different ways to "see" without using the eyes.

List the parts of a clock.................................

List all the ways to use a clock other than as a timepiece.

List three important things that happened in Humpty Dumpty's story. ....

List ways to put Humpty Dumpty together.

List five uses for a towel.................................

List many different ways to dry a towel.

List the original 13 colonies.................................

Rename the original 13 colonies if the Pilgrims landed at Los Angeles Rock.

List the parts of speech.................................

What might happen if people couldn't talk, read, or write?

▲ COMPARE/CONTRAST QUESTIONS

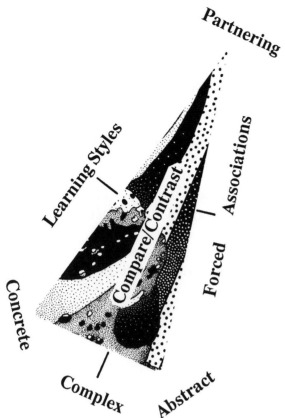

GOAL: To stimulate high level thinking

KEY: Forced Associations

Compare/contrast questions (how two things are alike and how they are different) are ideal examples of the development of a simple thinking process into a complex one. They move from the **concrete** to the **abstract**. In the following examples we compare/contrast two objects, ideas, or concepts from the same category. We gradually progress to more difficult/ **complex** categories that require **forced associations**.

Example: Ask students to choose partners. Have them hold out and examine their left hands. Ask **partners** to compare/contrast hands. Share responses with their partners.

How is _____ like _____ ?

How is _____ different from _____ ?

Note: The *"hands"* activity is great readiness. It also taps into different **learning styles** — the visual learners have something to look at, the kinesthetic learners have something to touch, and the auditory learners have something to say or hear.

The following compare/contrast topics can be practiced with a partner or in small groups.

left/ right hand	seeing/ believing	loafers/ high heels
knights/ nights	newspapers/ magazines	walking/ running
rain forest/ desert	ice cream/ frozen yogurt	landfills / time capsules
freedom/ boundaries	cars/ bicycles	human brain/ computers
building a building/ building a relationship		oranges/ apples
Clinton administration/Bush administration		Sega/hula hoops

History is filled with the appplication of compare/contrast questions and forced associations. My favorite example is the Quaker housewife who was sitting at her spinning wheel. She glanced out the window and saw her husband and a neighbor sawing a tree with a two-man crosscut saw. She compared the spinning wheel to the saw and — *voila!* She invented the circular saw. Forced association is the beginning of many inventions.

▼ COMPARE/CONTRAST CAREERS

An entire unit in career education can be developed around compare/contrast questions.

Bart Conner, the gymnast, was interviewed and written about in a teacher resource book. The unit about him began with guided imagery followed by the interview with Conner. The post interview activities included divergent questions. The unit also included a mindMap of the careers related to gymnastics. Questions for students included:

What if there had been no P.E. teacher interested in the gymnastics talent of Bart Conner?

What would it be like to be Bart Conner's younger brother Michael or older brother Bruce?

How would it feel to spend fourteen hours a day perfecting your skills?

List all the character traits a person should have in order to be in a profession that would put him in front of thousands of people every time he performed his skill.

Compare/contrast gymnastics with dance.

Compare/contrast gymnastics with gourmet cooking.

One important point: Move students from the *"How are they alike/different language"* to the words *compare/contrast.* Many achievement test questions use these words. Students may know how things are alike and different, but miss the compare/contrast questions because they are not familiar with the terms, are not taught the definitions, or are never given the chance to practice them.

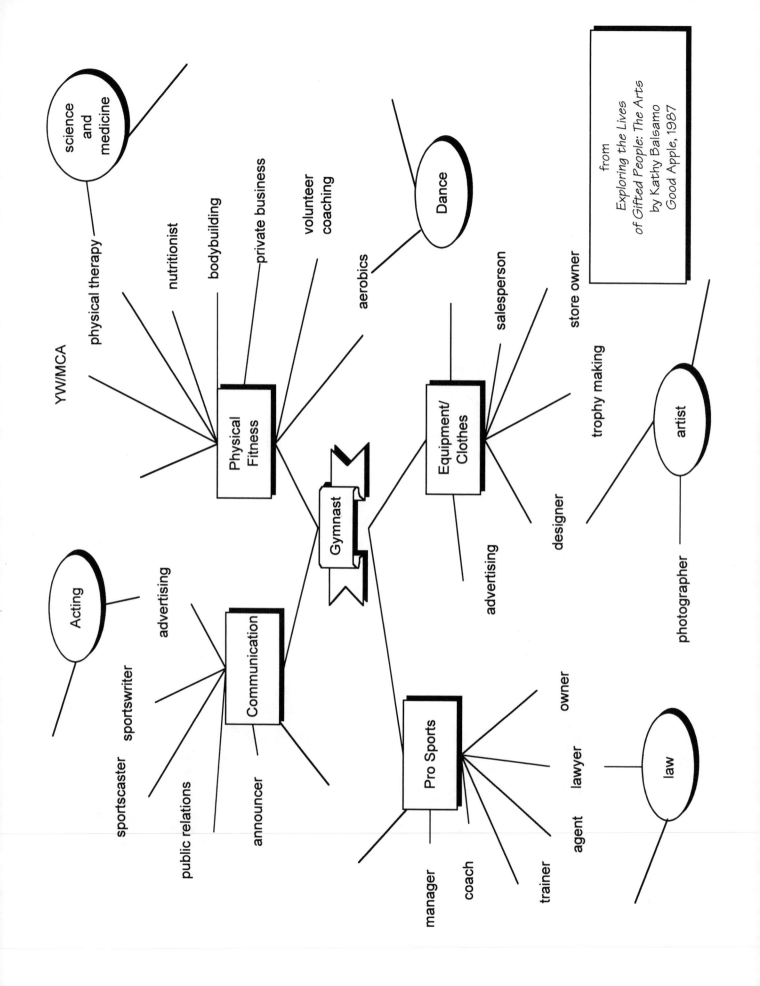

science and medicine

Dance

from
*Exploring the Lives
of Gifted People: The Arts*
by Kathy Balsamo
Good Apple, 1987

physical therapy

nutritionist

bodybuilding

private business

volunteer coaching

aerobics

YW/MCA

salesperson

store owner

trophy making

Physical Fitness

Equipment/Clothes

artist

designer

advertising

photographer

Gymnast

Acting

advertising

sportscaster

sportswriter

Communication

public relations

announcer

Pro Sports

owner

lawyer

law

manager

coach

trainer

agent

FEELINGS /OPINIONS /PERSONIFICATION QUESTIONS

GOAL: To motivate kids and their teachers
To value a child's opinion

KEY: Partnering

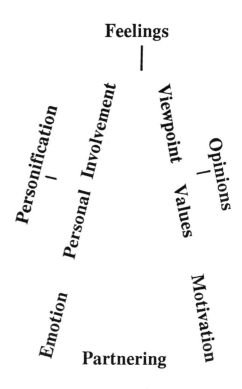

Experts say it isn't professional to single out one student as the teacher's pet. However, just this once, I must make an exception. Of the four questioning processes, this is my favorite. Feelings/Opinions/Personification questions are a powerful, exciting teaching tool for me. The truth is, I like these questions on a personal level. They are part of me, part of who I really am. I enjoy modeling these questions as well as teaching them.

Researchers characterize these as **viewpoint/ involvement** questions. They literally pull teacher and student together on an emotional level. And I like that.

There is an interesting *"fringe benefit"* with these questions. Feelings/Opinions/ Personification questions will open the door to **motivation.** The hidden force that motivates is **emotion.** These questions are charged with emotion, especially when they fit the student's age, interests, and abilities.

PARTNERING is the most effective way to introduce students to this form of questioning. It is easier to establish comfort level in partners than in groups. In the beginning it is best for the teacher to choose the partners and to switch partners every few minutes until students feel comfortable working with several different learning styles. The first examples begin at a low risk level that reinforces trust between the teacher/facilitator and student.

FEELINGS /OPINIONS: Are They One In The Same?

The words *feeling* and *opinion* are near-synonyms. However, in the questioning process it is necessary to separate them because it is possible to have strong feelings about something and not have an opinion. I may have strong feelings about abortion. On one hand, I may feel personal choice is paramount to our survival as a democracy. On the other hand, I may feel life is a precious gift to be nurtured and protected. I may not be able to formulate an opinion.

It is also possible to have an opinion about something and not have strong feelings. For example, in my opinion *Diet Pepsi* is better than *Diet Coke*. I really don't have strong feelings about that opinion. (I'll drink either one in a pinch!) That doesn't mean opinions are trivial. On the contrary, just ask me about one of my passionate causes, such as gifted children, and I'll cloud up and rain all over you with opinions and feelings!

▲ QUESTIONS ON THE MOVE: PREFERENCE

Have you heard? The brain is hooked to the body! More brain cells are stimulated when the human body is thinking on its feet. Remember some of those *"old fashioned"* teaching techniques: standing up to read, standing up to ask questions, standing up to answer. Maybe it's time to make standing up fashionable again.

Ask students to stand in a group in front of the teacher. The teacher begins the activity with the following instructions:

*"This activity is called **PREFERENCE**. Try to imagine that I am standing on a dividing line down the middle of the room. In just a moment I will ask all of you a question. You will show your answers by moving to either side of the dividing line. For example, if you could live in only one season of the year and your choices were winter (teacher points to left side of room) or summer (teacher points to right side of the room) which would you choose? Move to the side of the room that you prefer. Don't stand on the line. You may like both seasons or you may hate both. (Maybe spring is your favorite!) Try to choose anyway."*

After students have moved to the side they prefer, the teacher asks for oral responses. *"You have shown your opinion by moving to one side of the room. Can you support your opinion by sharing your reasons with the class?"* Do not expect all students to respond verbally. It is important to establish a fairly high comfort level, so don't put students on the spot by forcing them to answer. This activity not only gets kids up off their backsides, it gives even the shyest students the chance to participate by *"showing"* their opinions instead of voicing them.

NOTE: It is important that the teacher NOT give students permission to stand on the line. However, in some instances a student may either have very strong feelings about both or no feelings about either choice. Use this as a *"teachable moment."* Choosing not to choose is, in fact, a choice. This is the time a student must give strong, valid reasons for not choosing.

An alternative: Put vertical strips of tape on the floor, left to right, an equal distance apart. One end of the line of strips is designated *"stongly agree"* and the other is designated *"strongly disagree."* Students stand on one of the vertical tapes on the continuum where they are comfortable relative to the ends. Continue the activity by asking the following questions:

*Which season would you live in:
   Fall or Spring

*Would you rather wear:
   Gloves or Mittens

*Which tastes better:
   Pepsi or Coke

*Would you rather:
   Read the Book or See the Movie

*Which is more fun to do:
   Addition or Subtraction

*Which would you rather do:
   Write a Letter or Use the Phone

▼ QUESTIONS ON THE MOVE: PREFERENCE

YES!

- **Which cartoon would you rather watch:**

  POWER RANGERS or THE SIMPSONS

- **Which would you rather have for pets:**

  CATS or DOGS

- **Would you rather:**

  LEAD or FOLLOW

- **Which would you rather eat:**

  DILL PICKLES or SWEET PICKLES

- **Which would you rather have:**

  SPIKED HAIR or PIERCED EAR

- **If you played both well, which would you choose:**

  SOCCER or VOLLEYBALL

- **Which political party would you like to belong to:**

  DEMOCRAT or REPUBLICAN

- **Would you rather be:**

  A POSTCARD or LETTER

- **Would you rather be:**

  A FISHNET or A COBWEB

- **Which occupation would you rather be:**

  CHEF or VETERINARIAN

NO!

Place each choice on the continuum. Compare your preferences with your classmates.

▲ QUESTIONS ON THE MOVE: PREFERENCE

Where would you most like to spend your spare time:

OUTDOORS or INDOORS

Do you like to learn new things by:

HEARING or SEEING

Should a seat belt law be required in all states?

YES or NO

Would you rather live in:

A TREE HOUSE or A CAVE

Would you rather be:

A HIC-UP OR A BURP

Is it better to get the news by:

WATCHING TELEVISION or READING THE NEWSPAPER

Should the school day be lengthened one hour?

YES or NO

Suppose you were on the jury and you believed the crime justified it.
Would you vote for:

DEATH PENALTY or LIFE IN PRISON

As an occupation, would you rather be:

SKYSCRAPER WINDOW WASHER or UNDERGROUND MINER

▼ DEALING WITH STUDENT RESPONSES

Don't forget timing and comfort level. Students will respond more honestly if they **trust** the facilitator of the activity. Start with low risk choices such as the season of the year, foods, television shows, etc. Expect students to change their minds and switch sides during the activity. Discuss their reasons for doing so. (After all, don't we adults sometimes change horses in the middle of the stream?) Combining opinions and changing your mind is a true form of **synthesis**. **Listen** to their opinions. Expect strong emotions to surface as the high risk questions are asked. Be prepared to take TIME to help students **analyze** their choices and their feelings.

"Did you choose one side because you didn't like the other side?"

"Did you dislike both choices and the one you decided on was the lesser of two evils?"

"Did you wait for your best friend to choose and then you followed his/her lead?"

"How does it feel to be part of the majority/minority side?"

"Is it ok to have a different preference/opinion?"

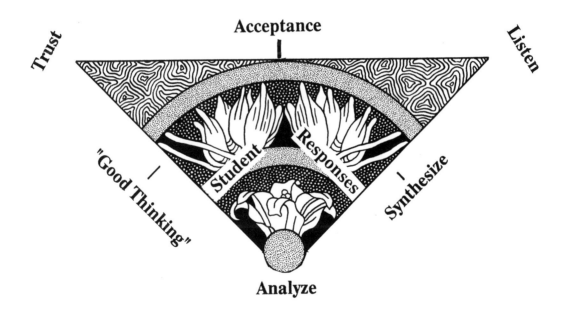

The word is **acceptance**. The Concept is AGREEING TO DISAGREE.

The teacher/facilitator must be careful not to *"beat a dead horse to death"* and over analyze each and every student response. Timing is important. Keep the activity moving.

In responding to unusual or divergent opinions use the response, ***"That's good thinking!"*** When the response is *'That's a good answer,'* the implication is it must be the right answer. And a right answer means there must be a wrong answer. That is NOT what this activity is about. There are no right or wrong answers in this activity, just answers—opinions and feelings. One final suggestion: the teacher/facilitator should withhold his/her personal opinions.

▲ WARNING! IT'S TIME FOR A REALITY CHECK!

The reason *Feelings/Opinions/Personification* questions are so motivating is they stimulate deep personal emotions. That in turn forces a re-examination of one's value system.

In my early teaching days, many school districts frowned on classroom teachers who explored values clarification questions. However, in my opinion, it is time to bring those questions back into active discussion. How can we discuss the dangers of drug and alcohol addiction and sexual promiscuity without valuing someone else's body or our own? Clarifying values makes students strong—hopefully, strong enough to deal with peer pressure and the challenge of being a responsible adult in an ever-changing frightening world.

BUT! Remember our schools reflect our communities. Teachers must take into consideration their important role as models for children as well as their position in the community.

On a few rare occasions, I stopped activities in my classroom because I was uncomfortable with the direction of a particular discussion. I simply said, *"Miss Johnson is feeling uncomfortable with this topic of discussion. We will stop this activity at this point. Please discuss the issue at hand with your parents. Tomorrow we will try to continue the discussion in a more comfortable direction."*

Does that sound cowardly? Maybe. Is that MY value system interfering? Maybe. The point is, I have to remember my responsibility as a professional educator who has the power to shape the minds of children. I don't like leaving children and adults on an emotional limb and then abandoning them. Besides that, my job might be on the line!

There certainly is no doubt about the power of personal opinion. Remember, if you encourage children to have opinions, they just might take you up on it.

Are you REALLY prepared to accept their opinions if they are different from your own?

▼ PERSONIFICATION QUESTIONS

What fun! To be able to speak for someone or something else — to see things from a DIFFERENT POINT OF VIEW. What if we gave the chair you might be sitting on a persona, a name, a personality? What would the chair have to say about having your body sitting on it? Sometimes architects give buildings a persona. Then they ask the building how it should be built. The following list of personification questions gives students practice in formulating viewpoints and opinions. Students may respond to a partner or write their ideas in a learning log or journal.

- You have just become a letter of the alphabet. Which letter are you? How do you feel?

- How would a butterfly feel about meeting a 747 airplane?

- If the color green could talk, what would it say about the color purple?

- The Brooklyn Bridge has been called by a local TV station to tell about its experiences. What is the bridge's version of its duties?

- How would you feel if you were a falling snowflake? How fast are you falling? Where are you going to land? Would you rather be a drop of rain?

- You are a wheelbarrow. Give a graduation speech for a class of building tools.

- What would Queen Victoria think about Bloomingdales?

- What would parallel lines say to vertical lines?

- Be a compass. Describe what you do. What kind of paper do you like to stick your point into? Do you ever get dizzy? What kind of pencil do you like to be paired with?

- How would Louis and Clark feel about a moon walk?

- You are a flag in the oval office of the White House. Describe what you see, hear, and smell.

- What questions would Louisa May Alcott ask Judy Bloome?

ACTIVE Personification Questions

Make a list of questions that:

Thomas Jefferson's quill pen might ask today's President.

✎ _____

a doctor's stethoscope might ask a disease.

✎ _____

the year 1812 might ask the year 2012.

✎ _____

a tiger in a zoo might ask a tiger in the wild.

✎ _____

a pair of worn-out shoes might ask Donald Trump.

✎ _____

the planet Mars might ask the planet Neptune.

✎ _____

oil might ask water.

✎ _____

the CIA might ask the KGB.

✎ _____

a picnic table might ask a library table.

✎ _____

a video game might ask a math textbook.

✎ _____

an obtuse triangle might ask a parallelogram.

✎ _____

wisdom might ask fear.

✎ _____

▼ Examples to use to create personification questions

What would this look like to a_____or a_____?

What would _____have done?

What would_____have thought?

How would this look to a _____?

What would a _____mean from the viewpoint of

a_____?

How would _____feel if it were human and could feel?

How would you feel if you were_____?

How might_____have said that?

Who might think differently about it?

_____

▲ WHAT WOULD HAPPEN IF...? QUESTIONS

GOAL: Creative Thinking   (Reorganization of Reality)

KEY: Laughter!

Did I write that *Feelings/Opinions/Personification* questions were my favorite? Well, actually, *"What Would Happen If . . . ?"* questions are my favorite. They are just plain fun! To completely let go of rigid thinking patterns, to break traditional mind sets, to open the mind to an ***"anything goes"*** *a*ttitude has to be one of life's greatest highs. The teacher who facilitates *what would happen if* questions must accept the responsibility as leader and **model for laughter** and **creative thinking** and questioning. "Seriosity" is a block to the whole process. Laughter is the key that unlocks divergence. Students need to see and analyze adults using the **divergent questioning** process. They also need guidance in moving from divergent thinking to convergent thinking.

Students can brainstorm in partners, small groups, journals, or learning logs . . . . .

What if each person had to have a 6 foot space around them at all times to survive?

What if Rogers had never met Hammerstein? Speilberg had not met Lucas?

What would happen if it were against the law to sing? to dance? to laugh?

What would happen if all the Pepsi in the world turned to water?

What if the human body needed to consume gold to survive?

What if Dr. Martin Luther King, Jr. had been born in 1840?

What would happen if your parents were movie stars?

What if all libraries were declared a health hazard?

What if human beings had never discovered fire?

What would happen if clothes never wore out?

What if a volcano erupted in your backyard?

What if the North Star were not stationary?

What if robots could own property?

What if spiders were insects?

Anything Goes
Brainstorming
Creative Thinking
Model
If
What Would Happen
Divergent Thinking
Laughter

 # WHAT IF . . .

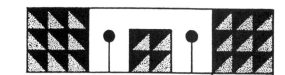

What if humans had x-ray eyes?

✐ _____

What if people could only travel in vertical lines? in ovals?

✐ _____

What would happen if all of a sudden you could not speak English?

✐ _____

What would happen if you were involved in a sit-down protest?

✐ _____

What if the Sumarians had not invented the arch?

✐ _____

What if it rained every Wednesday all over the world?

✐ _____

What would happen if your sneakers had wings?

✐ _____

What would happen if you could trade places with your parents?

✐ _____

What would happen if human beings had to sleep standing up?

✐ _____

What if time stood still on Tuesday morning at 11 AM?

✐ _____

What if your left hand was covered with velcro?

✐ _____

Adaptations of SCAMPER*
to create personification questions.

*A Good Resource
SCAMPER: Games for
Imagination Development
by Bob Eberle
D.O.K., 1971

- What would happen if_____?

- What would you do to _____if_____happened?

- In what other situation could_____?

- Let's pretend that_____?

- What if_____?

- Suppose_____. What would the consequences be?

- What if_____were_____?

- How would _____have been different if it were smaller? larger? stronger? heavier? sideways? upside down? a different color?

- How might things have changed if_____was reversed? rearranged? taken apart? more intense? of minor consequence?

- How would_____have been different if it had sound? lights? motion? an odor?

- What would happen if we put _____to other uses?

- What would happen if we took something away from_____and replaced it with_____?

- What would_____be like if the environment were changed to_____?

- How would _____react if _____existed in a different time period?

You are a QUILL PEN. The year is 1774.

Where are you? Who is your owner?

Describe how the bird felt who lost you.

Compare/contrast yourself to a ballpoint pen.

How does it feel to be dependent on an ink well?

What are all the things you can do besides make marks on a paper?

Describe an interesting experience that one of your famous ancestors had.

Your point has just broken. What is your fondest memory?

You are a STYROFOAM CUP in a landfill.

Describe your surroundings, including what you see, feel, and smell.

How were you used before you came to the landfill?

Describe your trip to the landfill. What were your feelings about being thrown away?

How does it feel to be pushed around by a bulldozer?

Do you ever get bored just laying around? What do you do for excitement?

What is your ultimate contribution to society?

There is a paper cup sitting next to you. The paper cup is dying. Write a conversation between the two of you. How long do you think you both will survive? What are your plans for the future?

You just found out that your landfill has been declared ecologically unsafe. Why? What happened? They are moving you to a new landfill. Where would you like to go?

Suppose you could escape the landfill. Where would you go and what would you be?

If you could send the children of the world a message about landfills, what would it say?

You are a Front SEAT IN A CITY BUS in Montgomery, Alabama. The year is 1955. A woman gets on the bus and sits down on you. Her name is Rosa Parks.

Describe how you look. Are there marks on you? Are there cuts and holes? Are you shiny and new?

It is the first time a black person has ever sat on you. How do you feel?

How is Mrs. Parks sitting on you? Can you feel what she is feeling?

How do the other seats react to what is happening? What do they say to you?

Do you think you are a special seat? Are you proud?

The Smithsonian called and wants to interview you and put you on display. What is your reaction?

Are there other famous seats you could compare yourself to?

Andy Worhal said, *"Everyone is famous for 15 minutes."* How does that apply to you?

WHAT WOULD HAPPEN IF . . . ?   THUMBS UP!

It is surprising how an entire unit of study can be built on just one question. ***Thumbs Up!*** begins with the question, *"What would happen if human beings did not have thumbs?"* First, students brainstorm the changes that would occur if human beings didn't have thumbs. This can be done in large groups, small groups, or partners. The facilitator encourages students to *"dig deep" for as many responses as possible.*

• ## Examples of changes and difficulties:

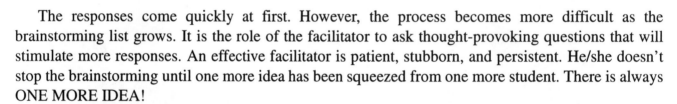

. . . gloves and mittens   . . . buttoning clothes

. . . holding a pencil for writing   . . . thumbing a ride

. . . playing some musical instruments   . . . sports and sporting equipment

. . . count by fours instead of fives   . . . shaking hands

The responses come quickly at first. However, the process becomes more difficult as the brainstorming list grows. It is the role of the facilitator to ask thought-provoking questions that will stimulate more responses. An effective facilitator is patient, stubborn, and persistent. He/she doesn't stop the brainstorming until one more idea has been squeezed from one more student. There is always ONE MORE IDEA!

Just when the students are about to give up and the frustration level is very high (*"Miss Johnson, our brains are dead! We can't think of anything else!"*) the facilitator presents two roles of masking tape. Tear the tape in 3 foot strips and tell the students to tape their thumbs down to the palms of their hands. Students can help each other.

Take the students on a school tour—Open doors, lockers, windows. Provide a box of "stuff" (scissors, bowling ball, jar of peanut butter with twist-on lid, eating utensils, and toys) and encourage students to experience a world without thumbs. Ask them to untie/tie shoes, button/unbutton clothes, and sharpen their pencils. Follow with more brainstorming.

It will amaze students and facilitator how many more ideas they are able to add to their list. Learning by doing stimulates thinking.

Thumbs Up! is the beginning of a unit on famous inventors and their inventions. After the taping, have students research inventions that require the human's opposing thumb. Because they have experienced not having thumbs they are keenly aware of its importance in the inventing process.

The culminating activity in the unit involves the students in redesigning something for a human hand without thumbs. What would a pair a scissors that is designed for a human hand without an opposing thumb look like? What would a bowling ball look like? Students will use the high level thinking processes of analysis, synthesis, and evaluation to complete their designs. And it all started with just one question!

▼ FLYING QUESTIONS!

There are many ways to practice the art of brainstorming. It can be done alone, in partners, small groups or large, written or oral, on paper, walls, or transparencies. It can be words, pictures, shapes, or all of the above. A simple and fun way to brainstorm different kinds of questions is to ask students to write an idea or subject at the top of an 8" x 11" piece of paper.

Then everyone folds their papers into paper airplanes.

* The teacher signals, GO! and the entire group flies their airplanes around the room.

* The teacher signals, STOP! Students pick up other students' airplanes, unfold them and write a divergent question on the paper about the subject written at the top of the page.

* The students then re-fold the airplanes, fly them again, and when they retrieve another airplane, they add a second question.

* The process is repeated several times. Each time students unfold airplanes they read several questions written by other students and then try to add a different one of their own. The activity is completed when students write a story or report about the topic and questions on one of the airplanes.

  More airplane ideas:

* Story Starters: Each student writes the beginning of a story on a piece of paper and folds it into an airplane. A "write, fold, and fly," pattern is established. After several repetitions of the pattern—voila! There is a story written by several people.

* Flying Math Problems: Students make up their own math worksheets and fold them into airplanes. Whoever gets the airplane completes those math problems.

* Airplane Spelling: Students choose words from a spelling list or dictionary that they know how to spell. They print them on an airplane. Whoever gets that list of words must learn how to spell them and then be tested by the writer of the list.

▲ Twenty Questions

Twenty Questions is a wonderful old-fashioned game to help students sharpen their questioning skills. It moves students toward personal inquiry which is the basis for active questioning. Students guess the identity of an object, idea, or person by asking questions that require only a yes or no response.

Twenty Questions stimulates active inquiry if students have the opportunity to play several times. So, be patient. Repeat the activity several times a week for several weeks. Active questioning takes practice!

▲ ACCOUNTABILITY

In business and industry it is called *"getting your ducks in a row"* or *"covering your backside."* In education it is called *accountability*. Educators must prove to the powers that be (administrators and school boards) how every dime, dollar, and minute is spent. Divergent questioning happens in most classrooms when the teacher feels confident and secure with the process and can show accountability.

A favorite accountability *"trick of the trade"* in the teaching profession is printing objectives on the chalkboard. It is amazing what a teacher can do if there is a list of objectives on the board!

QUESTIONING OBJECTIVES

1. The student will demonstrate an ability to articulate ideas clearly during partnering and/or group activities.

2. The student will demonstrate an ability to use social skills in participating in partnering and/or group activities.

3. The student will evidence an ability to interact easily with others by readily participating in the planned partnering and/or group activities.

4. The student will use convergent and divergent questions to undertake library research in order to gather data for the completion of assignments.

5. The student will use divergent questioning skills to apply, analyze, synthesize and evaluate printed materials to accomplish learning activities.

6. The student will use mindMaps to demonstrate organizational ability through the completion of an acceptable written composition.

7. The student will show an ability to appreciate the feelings and opinions of others by responding to divergent questions.

8. The student will use webbing and/or mindMapping to depict visually two remote or uncommon ideas.

9. The student will use convergent and divergent questioning skills to develop a more positive self concept by recognizing and using his/her abilities, becoming more self-directed and appreciating likenesses and differences between himself/herself and others.

10. The student will use convergent and divergent questioning skills to develop ideas related to broad-based issues, themes, or problems.

11. The student will stimulate high level thinking in himself/herself by being involved in an in-depth learning experience related to a self-directed topic.

12. The student will use divergent thinking to generate original ideas in completing a model, plan, or product that is unique.

13. The student will use convergent and divergent questioning skills to recognize the goals and objectives of a group by working toward consensus in cooperative learning situations.

14. The student will generate original convergent and divergent questions related to a topic or idea.

15. The student will brainstorm many responses that fit different categories.

16. The student will effectively interpret and use nonverbal forms of communication to express his/her ideas, feelings and needs to others.

17. The student will use active questioning techniques to describe his/her feelings and values.

18. The student will predict many different causes/effects for given situations by responding to convergent and divergent questions.

19. The student will respond to convergent and divergent questions by moving his/her body.

20. The student will stimulate high level thinking through kinesthetic experiences.

21. The student will use forced associations to stimulate high level thinking.

22. The student will show fluency by expressing many ideas though not all of the highest quality.

23. The student will show flexibility by expressing a variety of responses.

24. The student will show originality by expressing unusual, uncommon responses, though not all of the ideas prove to be useful.

25. The student will show elaboration by building onto or embroidering a basic idea by adding details to make it more interesting and complete.

Another accountability *"trick of the trade"* is the use of products. **Divergence** is more acceptable to some administrators when it leads to **convergence.** Consequently, teachers use the divergent questioning process with students who in turn use it to develop visible products. The following list of products are examples of what students can do with all those divergent responses.

PRODUCTS

Advertisement	Annotated Bibliography	Art Gallery
Collection	Chart	Cooperative Group Report
Choral Reading	Comic Strip	Computer Program
Creative Writing	Crossword Puzzle	Debate
Demonstration	Detailed Illustration	Diorama
Display	Drawing	Editorial
Essay	Experiment	Fact File
Fairy Tale	Family Tree	Filmstrip
Flip Book	Game	Graph
Hidden Picture	Illustrated Story	Interview
Labelled Diagram	Letter	Letter to the Editor
Learning Center	Map	Map with Legend
MindMap	Mobile	Model
Mural	Museum Exhibit	Newspaper Story
Oral Report	Pamphlet	Photo Essay
Pictures	Picture Story	Poem
Poster	Project Cube	Puppet
Puppet Show	Question Box	Rebus Story
Science Fiction Story	Sculpture	Shadow a Career for a Day
Skit	TV Play	TV/Radio News Script
Web	Write a Book	Write a Speech

The **teaching/learning process** breaks down if the teacher and learner do not APPLY the questioning techniques. Just as learning about riding a bicycle is not the same as actually riding one, LEARNING ABOUT questioning and actually LEARNING questioning are two very different things. The difference is application.

A near-synonym for application is **practice.** We just can't sugar-coat the process and expect good questioning to happen in one or two easy lessons. First, teachers must make a **commitment** to include **differentiated** questioning in their own thinking. Then, personal application is the best practice. Teachers will gain the confidence they need to use the skills in the classroom by using divergent questions to solve **personal** and work-related problems.

Another near-synonym for application is **infusion.** Differentiated questioning should never be taught in isolation. It is a way of thinking, a philosophy.

A few months ago, while fulfilling a consulting contract in a local school district, I asked the building administrator if her teachers were doing anything to improve questioning skills. She replied, *"Oh yes! We do that in the spring. We have a grant that is two weeks long. We do questioning in April!"* Making divergent questions part of every class, every subject, every day is what infusion really means.

In this section you will find excellent examples of the application and infusion of questioning from outstanding teachers and authors.

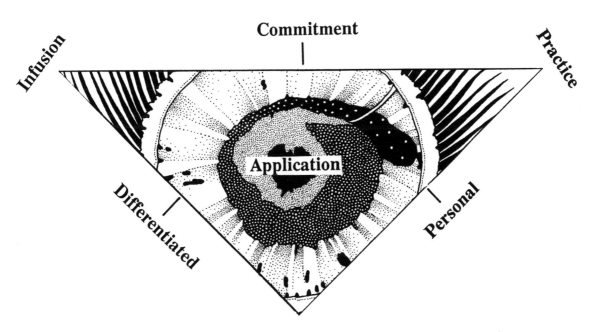

Teaching/Learning Styles

▲ Reading Charts

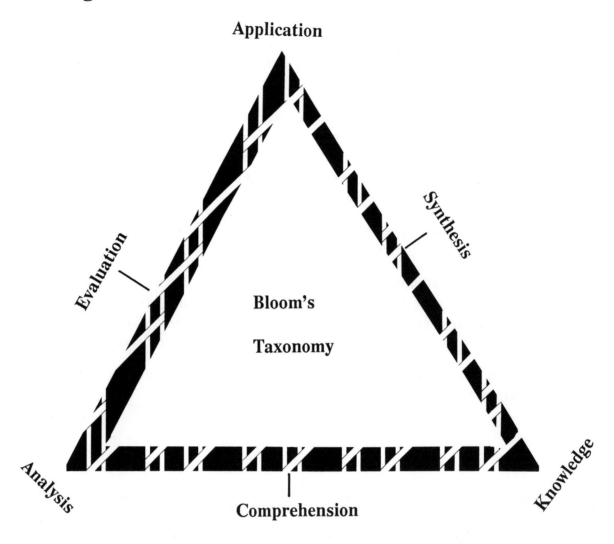

Application

Synthesis

Evaluation

Bloom's

Taxonomy

Analysis

Comprehension

Knowledge

SETTING

K   Where does the story take place?

C   Tell everything about the place where the story happens.

A   Describe a place that you've visited that is like the setting in the story.

AN   **List 3 ways the setting of this story is similar to and three ways it is different from where you live.**

S   **Design a poster encouraging people to visit the area where the story takes place. If the place has no name, create a name that you think fits the place.**

E   **Tell why you would or would not like to live where the story takes place.**

VOCABULARY

K   Find 5 words in the story that you do not know the meanings of.

C   Write a definition in your own words for each of the 5 words you picked.

A   Either draw or act out the definition for each of the 5 words.

AN   **For each of your 5 words, find 2 or 3 words that mean the same thing as the word you chose and that make sense in the story.**

S   **Pick 2 of your 5 words and create a word picture that uses the words as part of the picture and at the same time shows their meaning.**

E   **Using the numerals 1 through 5, rate the 5 words that you have chosen in the order of their importance to you (giving a 1 to the most important and a 5 to the least important). Be able to give reasons for your choices.**

CHARACTER

K   Who is the main character?

C   Write a short description of the main character, telling how he/she looks and acts.

A   Write a diary entry for 1 day that the main character would write.

AN   **Pick one of the characters in the story and write 5 questions that you would like to ask in order to understand the way he/she acted in the story.**

S   **Add a new adventure to the story involving the same characters that would make the story more exciting.**

E   **Pick any character in the story and tell why you think that character is the funniest, most likeable, bravest, least likeable, friendliest, most adventurous, most troublesome, or mischievous.**

CONTENT

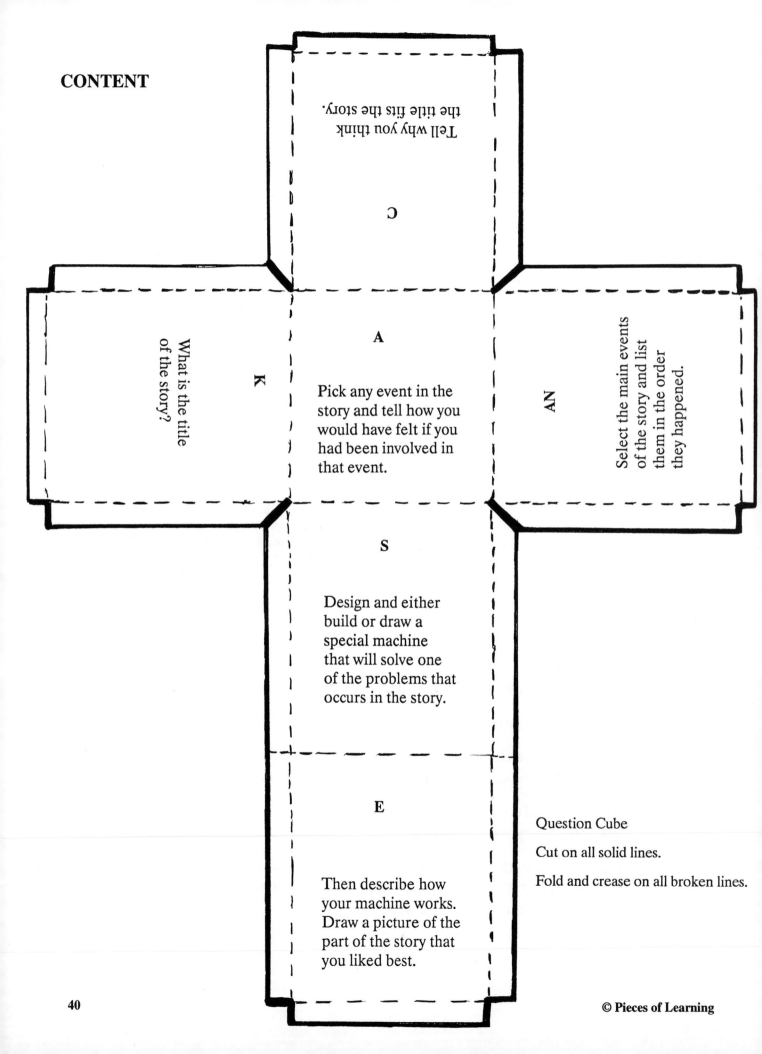

Tell why you think the title fits the story.

C

K

What is the title of the story?

A

Pick any event in the story and tell how you would have felt if you had been involved in that event.

AN

Select the main events of the story and list them in the order they happened.

S

Design and either build or draw a special machine that will solve one of the problems that occurs in the story.

E

Then describe how your machine works. Draw a picture of the part of the story that you liked best.

Question Cube

Cut on all solid lines.

Fold and crease on all broken lines.

▼ The Social Studies Question Is . . .

1. Use triangles to tell what you think of when you hear the word "imperialism."

2. Paint a picture that shows the meaning of "dollar diplomacy."

3. Draw a cartoon and write a caption for it showing the attitude of most Americans toward the war in Europe in 1915.

4. Prepare a 1-page activity dealing with the "open-door" policy. Exchange the activity with a partner and complete his/her activity.

5. Pretend you are a lamp in the Oval Office during Theodore Roosevelt's administration. Write a 1-page essay telling what you would see and hear during one of TR's foreign policy decisions.

6. In small groups, produce and present a 12-minute TV news broadcast of present-day foreign policies. Videotape the program and play it for the class.

7. What would have happened if the United States had not used the atomic bomb in World War II?

8. Find 25 pictures and write captions for each to describe the foreign policies of Ronald Reagan's administration.

9. Find 12 headlines from today's newspaper that could have appeared in American newspapers in 1941. Be able to explain how.

10. Find 10 job want ads in today's newspaper that could be involved in some way with our foreign policy today. Explain how.

11. Write headlines for each of 6 current foreign affairs newspaper articles.

12. Write articles for each of 4 foreign affairs headlines from today's newspaper.

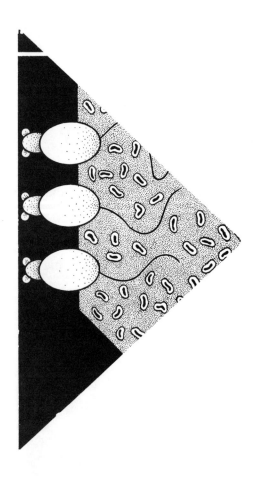

13. Write 2 one-page editorials—one favoring our action in Vietnam or Panama, and one opposing our action there.

14. Prepare some propaganda—one set favoring American support and aid to the Allies in 1940 and one set opposing any aid to a belligerent power.

15. In small groups you must unanimously agree or disagree with 6 controversial statements about a peace-time draft.

16. Arrange in chronological order a series of 10 pictures about the Cold War.

17. Complete a chart about American industry. Then develop 6 questions to go with the chart.

18. Classify 20 given words or phrases dealing with American neutrality in 4 different ways.

19. Try to "stump the expert" (the teacher or another student) with questions about World War II.

20. Write 1-3 sentences (using only song titles) to describe Harry Truman's foreign policy.

21. If you were writing a book "The Causes of World War II" list 6 chapter titles you would use. Write 2-4 sentences telling why you used each title.

22. Rank the 20th Century American presidents in order of their success with foreign policy. In small groups reach unanimous agreement as to a ranking. Then as a class, reach unanimous agreement as to a final ranking.

23. Of the 5 causes of World War I which was the most important in causing the United States to declare war on Germany in 1917? Write a 1-page essay telling why you chose that cause.

24. Write 12 statements dealing with JFK's foreign policy. Some statements should be fact and some opinion. Exchange papers with a partner and mark each statement as fact or opinion. Check your answers with the statement's author.

25. Write 6 paragraphs dealing with Jimmy Carter's foreign policies. Some paragraphs should be objective and some should have a bias flavor. Exchange papers with a partner and mark each paragraph as being objective or bias. Check your answers with the paragraph's author.

26. Individually, with a partner, or in a group of 3 or 4, write and record a song that gives the feeling of the times in early December, 1941.

27. Use your other subject textbooks to find titles or subtitles that could be used in a book entitled *20th Century Foreign Policy*. Be able to tell how each title could be used.

28. List alternatives to solve the American hostage crisis. Rank the best 5 and defend your ranking.

29. Select a popular comic strip for one week. Block out what was said by the characters. Then write your own comments so the comic strip describes one phase of Dwight Eisenhower's foreign policies.

30. With a partner, use the items in a paper sack (pencil, string, bottle cap, etc.) to describe one phase of Woodrow Wilson's foreign policies.

31. From the remains of a partially burned letter from a Secretary of State, name the Secretary of State, his boss, and prepare 6 questions about their foreign policies.

32. Suppose a group of Soviet high school students were visiting your city in the period from 1945-1953. Make a list of 10 questions you would expect them to ask and the answer you would give them.

33. What color or colors do you think an abstract painter would use to paint a picture of American foreign policy under Richard Nixon? Write a paragraph explaining your choices.

34. Write a recipe for the making of an American President. Include at least 6 ingredients. Write 2-4 sentences explaining your reasons for including each ingredient.

35. Select 10 song titles that describe U.S. foreign policy in the 1950s and 1960s. Write 2-4 sentences explaining your reasons for including each.

36. As a magazine writer you have been assigned to write an article describing American foreign policy under George Bush. You will need cartoons and pictures for the article. Therefore, you need to write instructions to the staff cartoonist and photographer telling them the type of information that should be in 2 cartoons and 4 pictures that they are to supply for your article.

37. If you are going to field a baseball team made of 20th Century American presidents (based on their foreign policy achievements), which man would you assign to each of the 9 positions on the field? Which 7 men would you keep on the bench? Write 2-4 sentences about each man telling why you managed the team as you did.

38. You are the producer-director of a new television series. Name the show. Tell what characters each of the 20th Century American presidents play. Write 2-4 sentences giving your reasons for your role selections.

39. Draw 4 inferences and make 4 predictions from 3 pictures of scenes from the 1950s.

40. You are planning a meal for the presidents of the 20th Century. However, you may seat only 3 people at each table. Draw a map of your seating arrangements, and explain why your tables are arranged as they are, and why you have seated the presidents as you have.

41. Write a one-page essay either agreeing or disagreeing with the statement—"U.S. presidents should be given another 4 years in the White House after already serving 8 years as president of the United States."

42. List the 6 personality characteristics you feel are most important for a president of the United States. Then observe people. Find someone who appears to have the characteristics you chose. Discuss your experience with the class.

43. Drop a blob of red, yellow and brown paint on a piece of paper. Fold the paper and blot the paint. Open the paper and study your results. Which phase of John Kennedy's foreign policy does it make you think of? Explain your reasons to the class.

44. Work with a partner (girl-boy). Pretend you are a 20th century president and his wife. Converse about the successes and failures of your foreign policy. The class will guess your identity.

45. Small groups will be given 2 words. The group must write a short story about the Monroe Doctrine using the 2 words. Pass the story to the next group. They write a problem based on the story. Pass the story to the next group. They write a solution to the problem. Pass the story to the next group and they write a moral to the story. Then read the paper to the class.

46. Write 5 questions on 5 separate sheets of paper. Shuffle them. Give your 5 questions to a classmate (face down—no one is to look at the questions until told to do so). At the teacher's signal, turn over the 1st question and begin writing a story using that question about U.S. neutrality in the 1930s. Do not stop writing to think—keep writing. After 3 minutes, turn over the second question and incorporate it into your story. Repeat this for the 3rd, 4th, and 5th questions. Read your story to the class and students will attempt to guess which questions were given to you.

47. Prepare a front page for an American newspaper for December 7, 1941. Do the same for a Japanese newspaper for the same day.

48. Using 5 of 8 given words associated with the foreign policy of one of our presidents since 1945 write a paragraph showing a relationship between the words.

49. Write a radio speech for FDR. Give his position on neutrality in February, 1941.

50. Find 10 sentences in today's newspaper that might have been used to describe President Johnson's foreign policy. Tell the class how each statement describes the policy.

51. Pretend you are a newly elected president currently in the process of naming your cabinet. List necessary characteristics for the posts of Secretary of State and Secretary of Defense. Who would you select from the class to fill the positions? Tell why you selected those you did.

52. Write a radio script for Robin Williams and a guest. The show is to be aired in 1943 from the deck of a U.S. aircraft carrier in the Pacific. Broadcast the script over the PA system.

53. You and 5 of your classmates have been placed in a "Think Tank" at the Department of State. You are to formulate a policy for the President to follow if the Soviets send troops to rebuild the Berlin Wall. Prepare a formal-looking document with your recommendations for the president.

54. Draw a picture of Adolf Hitler's personality. Explain your drawing to the class.

55. Pretend the Vietnam War is a boxing match, and you are the announcer. Describe how you would call the fight.

Thank you to Roy Martin, Social Studies teacher, for sharing these questions.

Use these nine school calendars to promote and practice questioning skills and thinking. Students can work in groups or individually to respond. Questions can motivate projects. And students can add questions to share with the class. Duplicate the calendars to include in journals. Students can use these ideas in their writing.

Monday	Tuesday	Wednesday	Thursday	Friday
	List the ten most important words to a mother. Dramatize them.		List things with wrinkles.	
		Make a list of funny words. Compare them with classmates.		List ways to make someone move.
Combine a paper clip and a ribbon. Draw your idea.				
		Make a set of 10 sentences that follow this pattern: ___ is bad, but ___ is worse.		Imagine a cold, dark, dreary day. What are your feelings? What are you doing?

Monday	Tuesday	Wednesday	Thursday	Friday
List your ideas about cooperation.			Show how a sentence is like a building.	Compare/contrast a snowflake and a raindrop.
	How is mathematics like color? How is it different?			
Ask several "where" questions about humor.			List symbols of power.	
		List your ideas about patterns.		Combine a hose and a wagon. Draw your idea.

Monday	Tuesday	Wednesday	Thursday	Friday
		Would you rather be a hiker or a biker?		List ways to capture an ant.
	What questions can you ask about mud?			
Would you rather be a pencil or paper? Why?		What is over the rainbow?		
			How is a student like a lamp?	
	How is a toothpick like a pickle?		Key is the answer. What could the questions be?	

48

Monday	Tuesday	Wednesday	Thursday	Friday
Name things with angles.				
		How is a classroom like an envelope?		How is an orange like a violin?
		List uses for a hair dryer.		
	What jobs are related to the color green?			
		List things you can do in a minute or less.		What if all roads were one way?

Monday	Tuesday	Wednesday	Thursday	Friday
List reasons for walls.				How are restaurants like toy shops?
			Compare/contrast your favorite TV shows.	
List things that are uneven.		How is a bird like a circle?		
	What did silver say to black?			
		Write new ways to make one hundred.	Compare/contrast silence and sound.	

Monday	Tuesday	Wednesday	Thursday	Friday
What is free? Explain your responses.		Compare/contrast two "Thanksgiving" food dishes.		Ask a "what" question about change.
	How is science like a drama?	Ask a "why" Question about time.		
				List things that can fit into a thimble.
		Design a new use for a sprinkler.		
			Compare/contrast hands and feet.	

© Pieces of Learning

Monday	Tuesday	Wednesday	Thursday	Friday
		What is inside the box? Web your ideas.		
What if all timepieces disappeared?			Would you rather meet a singer or a painter? Why?	
	What did the key say to the lock?			What if you could fly?
List things that go around.				
		List questions you might ask a builder.	What would a hammer say?	

52

Monday	Tuesday	Wednesday	Thursday	Friday
For what would you want to be famous? Why?		What makes something a problem?		Would you rather be courageous or inventive?
	Would you rather go left or right?			
Would you rather be too full or too empty?			What is heavier-- Monday or Saturday?	
	How are schools like amusement parks?			List problems a grocer might have.

Fill in the boxes with good questions. Use yours and your students'. Have a class discussion, use in a journal, and discuss at home.

Monday	Tuesday	Wednesday	Thursday	Friday

▼ Was It Possible?

Motivate students to sharpen their research skills with questions that stimulate curiosity. Each question requires the student to locate two dates. Answers are given in parentheses. Your students may find different answers!

1. Was it possible for Pocahontas to gaze at the stars through a telescope? (Yes, the telescope was invented in 1608, nine years before her death in 1617.)

2. Was it possible for Davy Crockett to send a letter via the Pony Express? (No, Crockett died in 1836. The Pony Express was not in operation until 1860.)

3. Was it possible for Queen Victoria to fasten her gown with a zipper? (Yes, the zipper was invented in 1893. Victoria didn't die until 1901.)

4. Was it possible for Mark Twain to watch the film version of Huckleberry Finn on television? (No, TV was invented in the 1920s at least ten years after Twain's death in 1910.)

5. Was it possible for Christopher Columbus to fire a cannon? (Yes, the cannon was invented in 1350, more than 100 years before Columbus' voyage to America.)

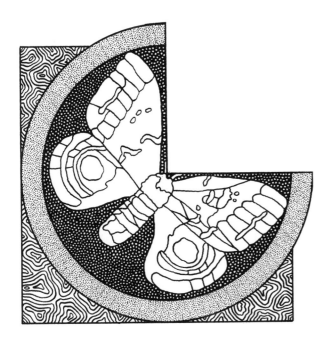

6. Was it possible for the Scottish novelist Sir Walter Scott to type his novels on a typewriter? (No, Scott died in 1832, thirty-five years before the invention of the typewriter.)

7. Was it possible for William Shakespeare to use a thermometer to find out the temperature? (Yes, the thermometer was invented in 1593. Shakespeare died in 1616.)

8. Was it possible for John F. Kennedy to watch shots of the first moon landing on TV? (No, Kennedy was assassinated in 1963. Man did not land on the moon until 1969.)

9. Was it possible for Sitting Bull to send a postcard to General George Custer before the Battle of Little Bighorn? (Yes, postcards were first issued in 1873, about three years before the 1876 massacre.)

10. Was it possible for Dolly Madison to fasten her skirt with a modern safety pin? (Yes, it was possible but not likely. Walter Hunt patented the safety pin in 1849, the same year Mrs. Madison died.)

11. Was it possible for Thomas Jefferson to shave with a safety razor? (No, Jefferson died in 1826, while the safety razor wasn't invented until 1903.)

12. Was it possible for Lewis and Clark to use a lead pencil to record their expedition across the Rocky Mountains? (Yes, the lead pencil was invented about 1650. Lewis and Clark explored the west in 1804-1806. American-made pencils, however, were not sold until 1812.)

13. Was it possible for Walt Disney to draw his first pictures of Mickey Mouse with a ball-point pen? (No, Disney created Mickey Mouse in 1928. The ball-point pen came into existence in 1938.)

14. Was it possible for Emperor Napoleon III to ride a pedal bicycle? (Yes, the pedal bicycle was invented in France in 1866 during Napoleon III's reign.)

15. Was it possible for Richard the Lion-Hearted and his crusaders to sail on a three-masted ship? (No, Richard reigned from 1189 to 1199. Three-masted ships were not produced until 1450.)

16. Was it possible for Sequoya to take a photograph of his Cherokee alphabet? (Yes, photography was invented in 1826. Sequoya died in 1843.)

17. Was it possible for William McKinley to fly in an airplane or a helicopter during his term in office? (No, McKinley was President from 1897 to 1901. The airplane wasn't invented until 1903, and the helicopter wasn't invented until 1907.)

18. Was it possible for Marie Antoinette to fly in a lighter-than-air balloon? (Yes, the first manned balloon flight occurred in France in 1783, ten years before her death.)

19. Was it possible for Leif Ericson to use a magnetic compass on his voyages? (No, Ericson's voyages took place about 990-1000. The magnetic compass wasn't invented until 1100.)

20. Was it possible for Napoleon's doctor to examine him with a stethoscope? (Yes, Napoleon died in 1821, five years after the invention of the stethoscope in 1816.)

21. Was it possible for Abraham Lincoln to send a Presidential message via the Pony Express? (Yes, Lincoln was inaugurated on March 4, 1861. The Pony Express was in existence until October 24, 1861.)

22. Was it possible for Mrs. Coolidge to serve commercially frozen food to guests at the White House? (Yes, frozen foods were first marketed in the 1920s. Calvin Coolidge was President from 1923 to 1929.)

23. Was it possible for Aesop to write his fables on paper? (No, paper as we know it wasn't invented until 105. Aesop died about 560 B.C.)

24. Was it possible for Marco Polo to go skiing? (Yes, skis had been in use since 1200. Marco Polo lived from 1254 to 1324.)

25. Was it possible for Americans to enjoy Coca-Cola during the first American motion picture? (Yes, Coca-Cola was patented in 1886. The first motion picture took place in 1896.)

Active Questioning:
Encourage students to write their own *"Was It Possible"* questions.

These questions first appeared in Challenge magazine. They were written by a prolific and gifted educator, the late Kelly Riley. Her mother graciously granted permission to use these questions.

"Seeing" Questions

Questioning can easily become a visual activity by using a teaching technique called webbing or **mindMapping.** MindMapping begins with simple **brainstorming** techniques. It presents a visual **framework** for those ideas from which a product is produced. The MindMap allows fantasy and imagination, language rhythms, patterns, associations, and metaphors to emerge into an organizational framework.

Sometimes in the brainstorming process while questions and responses are being placed on the mindMap, the student has an "aha" experience and a topic or central idea emerges.

Students who are visual learners will appreciate *"seeing"* their questions and responses on a mindMap.

It's About Writing is an excellent collection of mindMaps. A few examples follow.

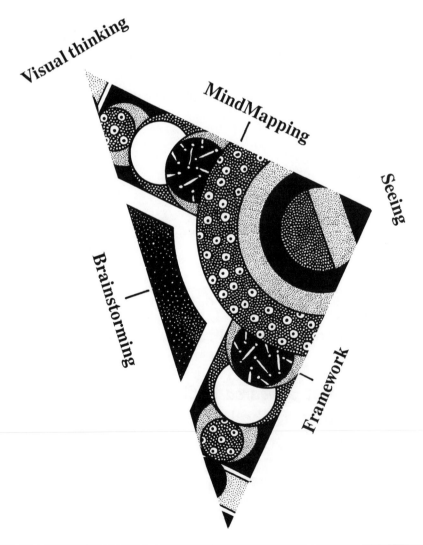

Webbing

A Good Resource
It's About Writing
Kathy Balsamo
Pieces of Learning, 1990

Closing Our School In Our Community

Fill in the links with reasons NOT to close your school and force students to go to other schools in your school district or to neighboring communities. Then write a letter to the newspaper editor, "Dear Editor: We do not want to be forced to another school because..." Use your links to explain why you do not think your school should be closed.

From a Good Resource
© 1990 It's About Writing,
Kathy Balsamo
Pieces of Learning,
Beavercreek OH

Animal Report

Fill in the links with ideas you want to investigate about your topic.

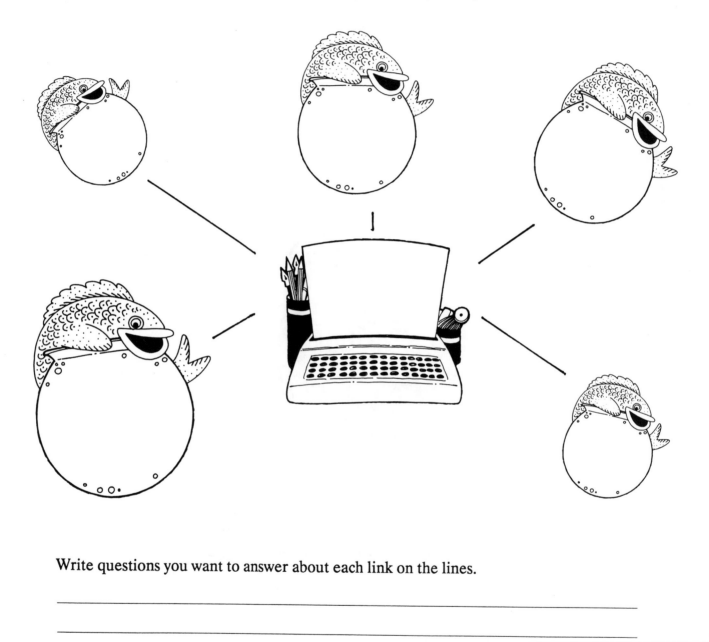

Write questions you want to answer about each link on the lines.

_____

_____

_____

_____

_____

From a Good Resource
© 1990 It's About Writing, Kathy Balsamo, Pieces of Learning, Beavercreek OH

Book Shares

Many students resist oral presentations because they haven't had consistent opportunities to make "stand up" deliveries followed by encouragement and suggestions. Using literature as a motivator, a bookshare mindMap will give students a handle on their way to improving their oral presentations.

The mindMap helps students organize thoughts about a book. Students manipulate ideas and put them into an **interesting sequence (outline)** or create a **unique approach** or **point of view** to the story using the visual framework.

Have students chose the focus for the book they are reading. Have the teacher choose the framework (that is the number of **links, elaboration lines,** and **bridges**). Have students develop sentences and then create a paragraph. The **focus** is the subject of the topic sentenc.

If students use more than one **focus** , they may develop each into a paragraph and sequence the paragraphs into a written or oral bookshare to give to the class. Focus ideas may include:

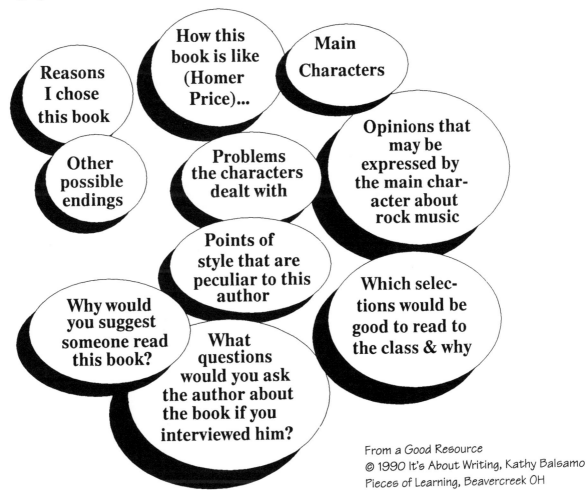

From a Good Resource
© 1990 It's About Writing, Kathy Balsamo
Pieces of Learning, Beavercreek OH

Thinking Diffferently about Math

Do some different kind of thinking. Write a word problem that goes with this mindMap.

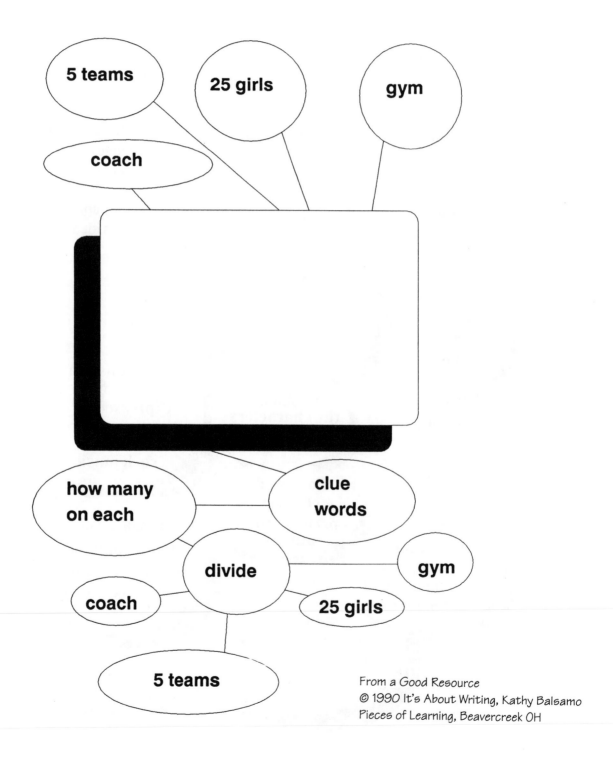

From a Good Resource
© 1990 It's About Writing, Kathy Balsamo
Pieces of Learning, Beavercreek OH

List things related to mathematics. MindMap your ideas.

What is a hermit? What advantages do you see in being a hermit?

The answer is "school." What are some questions?

List occupations of people who make a living with their mouths.

Which would you rather be, a monkey or an elephant?

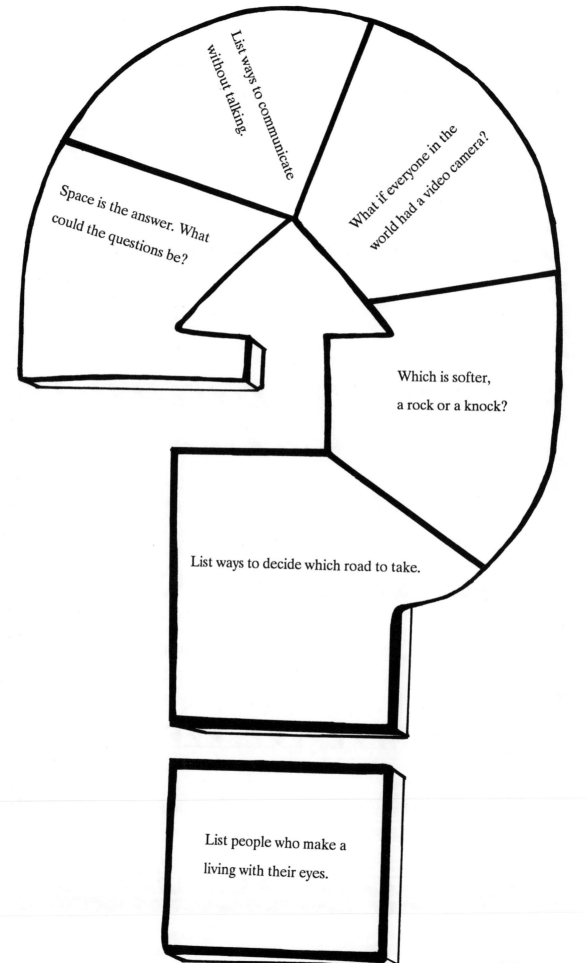

List ways to communicate without talking.

What if everyone in the world had a video camera?

Space is the answer. What could the questions be?

Which is softer, a rock or a knock?

List ways to decide which road to take.

List people who make a living with their eyes.

Ask several "when" questions about air.

Would you rather be a piano or a paintbrush? Why?

Write a letter to a current world leader. Express an opinion about his/her country.

List ideas that come to mind when you hear the world "crunch."

Compare/contrast something old with something new.

Compare/contrast lakes and rivers. Illustrate your ideas.

The answer is "round." What are the questions?

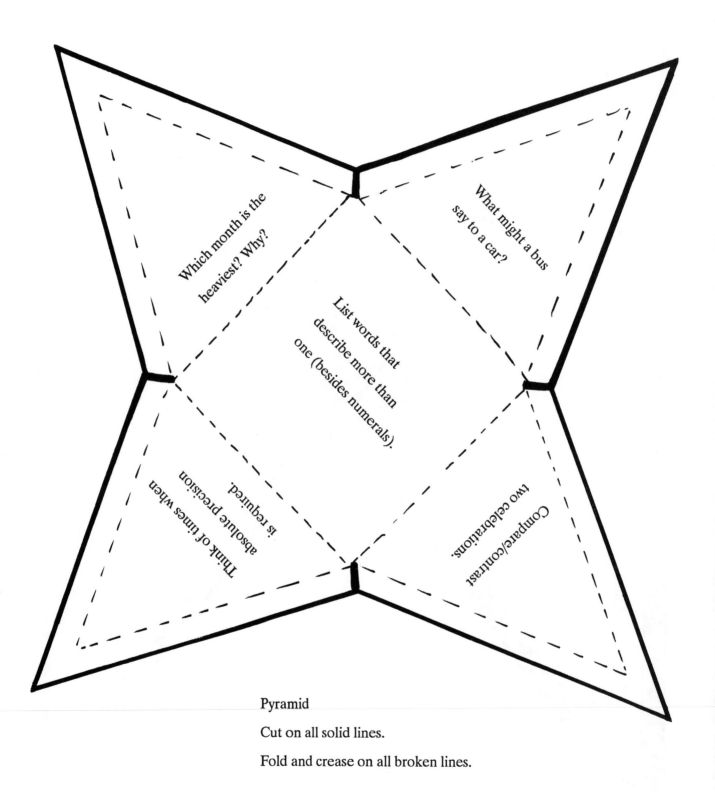

Which month is the heaviest? Why?

What might a bus say to a car?

List words that describe more than one (besides numerals).

Think of times when absolute precision is required.

Compare/contrast two celebrations.

Pyramid

Cut on all solid lines.

Fold and crease on all broken lines.

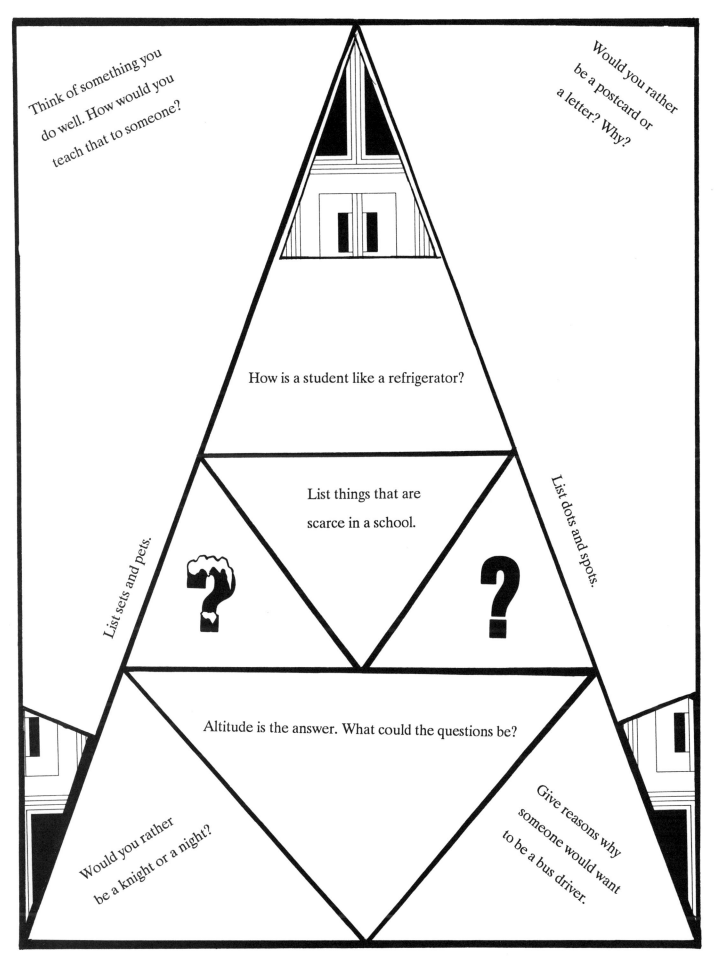

Think of something you do well. How would you teach that to someone?

Would you rather be a postcard or a letter? Why?

How is a student like a refrigerator?

List things that are scarce in a school.

List sets and pets.

List dots and spots.

Altitude is the answer. What could the questions be?

Would you rather be a knight or a night?

Give reasons why someone would want to be a bus driver.

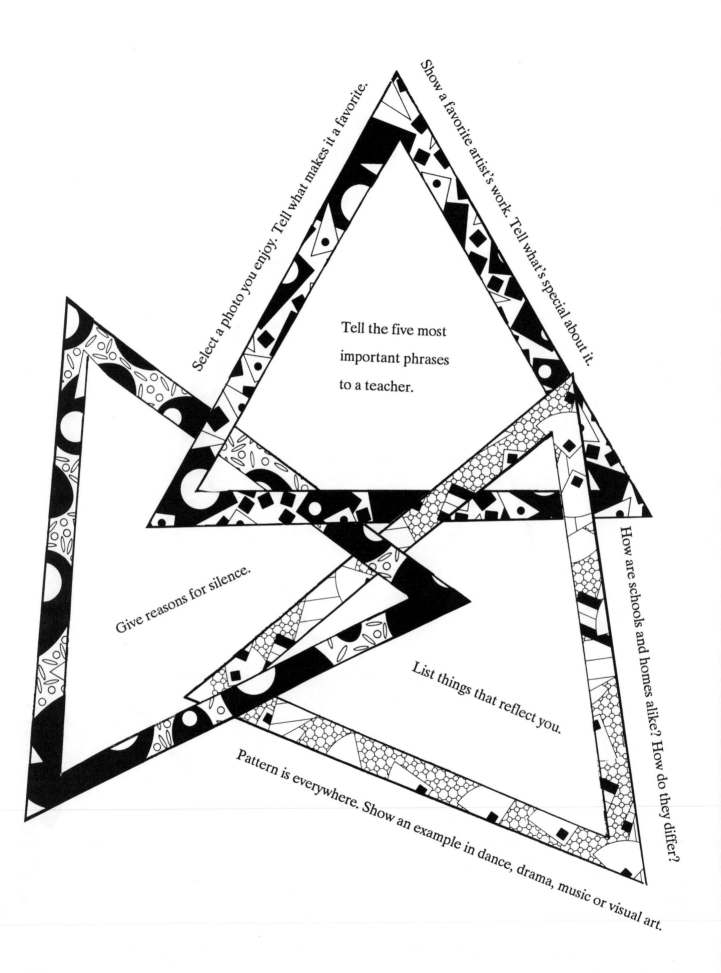

Select a photo you enjoy. Tell what makes it a favorite.

Show a favorite artist's work. Tell what's special about it.

Tell the five most important phrases to a teacher.

Give reasons for silence.

How are schools and homes alike? How do they differ?

List things that reflect you.

Pattern is everywhere. Show an example in dance, drama, music or visual art.

Thank you to Janice Szabos,
Fairfax County Gifted Coordinator,
for sharing questions for the calendar section,
originally appearing in *Challenge* magazine,
and questions for the "Seeing" section.

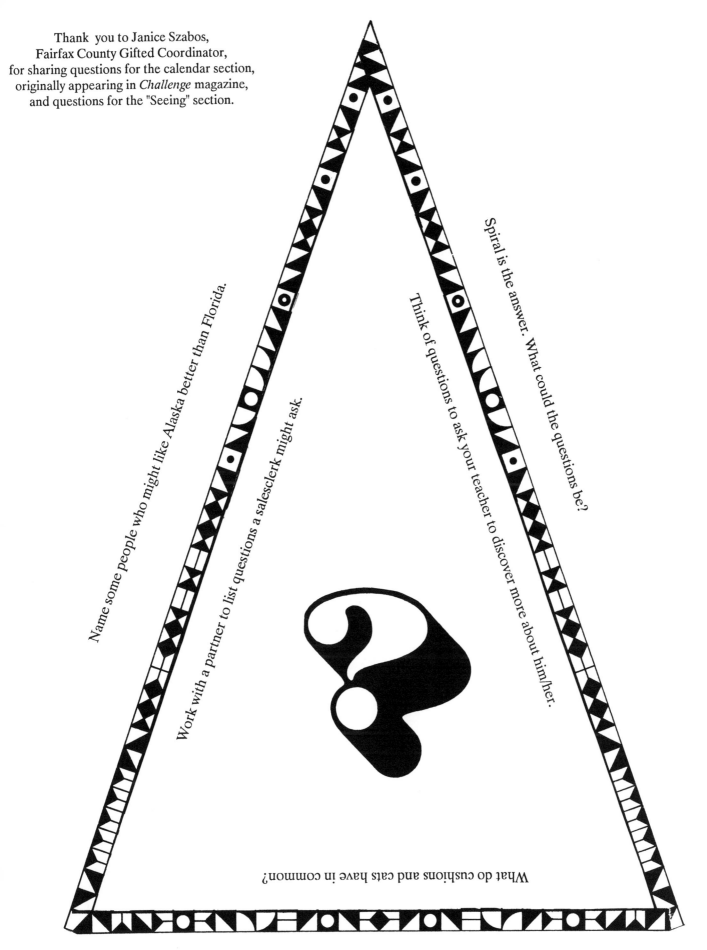

Spiral is the answer. What could the questions be?

Think of questions to ask your teacher to discover more about him/her.

Name some people who might like Alaska better than Florida.

Work with a partner to list questions a salesclerk might ask.

What do cushions and cats have in common?

What are some advantages and disadvantages of living on an island?

Math Questions
Across the Curriculum

No, this is not an April Fool's Day joke!

The leatherback turtle is one of nature's larger animals. These turtles are found in the Pacific Ocean and weigh up to 1,000 pounds. An adult turtle is 6 to 7 feet in length. One turtle, caught off the coast of Monterey, California, in 1961, weighed 1,906 pounds. It was 8'4" long. **How much more does the Monterey turtle weigh than you?**

How is a turtle like a beach ball?
Make a list of names for these gigantic turtles.
What if turtles lived in trees?
Make a mobile of other animals that weigh over 1000 pounds.

April 2

Hans Christian Anderson was born today in 1805.

His father was a shoemaker and made Hans wooden shoes to wear. Hans Christian Anderson wrote over 160 fairy tales. Some of his stories were about his own life. Two of his famous ones were *"The Ugly Duckling"* and *"The Princess and the Pea."* Hans also wrote plays and novels. In 1835, he wrote his first fairy tale. **How old was he?**

List characters that you could write a fairy tale about.

_____   _____   _____

_____   _____   _____

Pick one and write a tale "A Shoe for _____"
Read "The Ugly Duckling."
How would you feel if you had been the ugly duckling's friend?

_____

_____

_____

_____

_____

April 3

The Pony Express began in 1860.

Horseback riders rode as fast as they could to carry U.S. mail. The route, from St. Joseph, Missouri, to Sacramento, California, followed the Oregon-California Trail. Fresh horses were kept at relay stations about 10 to 15 miles apart. The very first Pony Express trip took 10 days and covered 1,966 miles. **If 26 riders went on the first trip, estimate how many miles each rider rode?.**

How is a Pony Express rider like a postcard?
List names that the riders might have called their horses.
Why was it called the Pony Express?
Draw a map (with a legend and key) for a Pony Express rider from your town to the next nearest town.

April 4

Linus Yale, American inventor, was born in 1821.

Linus Yale, Jr., invented the cylinder lock in 1860. He worked with his father to develop locks for banks. Most early locks were not as secure or as small as the Yale lock. Each lock contained a bolt that moved in and out of a slot. The Yale's lock was more complicated and therefore more efficient. **If you had a front door and a back door plus a basement door and a garage door, how many locks would you need to put one on each door?**

Why was the lock an important invention?
Name all the keys that you can.
What other ways can you "lock" something up?
What is a locket?
Draw a picture of something you have "locked" in your heart.

April 5

Tina Maria Stone set a record for a long distance run.

Tina Stone was born in Naples, Italy. When she came to the United States, she moved to California with her family. She became a long distance runner and set a record for running 15,472 miles in one year. **How many miles did she average each week?**

How is a runner like a string bean?
Time some of your friends as they run 25 yards.
Chart the results.

Harry Houdini, a famous magician, was born in 1874.

Mr. Houdini's real name was Ehrich Weiss and he grew up in Wisconsin. His parents came from Budapest, Hungary. He loved to do magic tricks and became famous for his daring underwater escapes. Harry began performing magic tricks when he was 17 years old in New York City. **If Mr. Houdini did 6 magic tricks every 5 minutes for an hour, how many tricks would he do all together?**

How is a magician like a racehorse?
Interview Mr. Houdini after he has completed one of his daring underwater escapes.
Design a poster advertising his magic show.

April 7

An enormous chocolate Easter egg was made.

The ostrich and the hummingbird lay nature's largest and smallest eggs. An ostrich egg weighs about 3 1/2 pounds and a hummingbird's egg weighs less than an ounce. This man-made chocolate Easter egg weighed 7,561 pounds and 13 1/2 ounces and was made in England. The egg measured 10 feet high. **Estimate how many ounces more an ostrich egg weighs than a hummingbird egg.**

Name things that weigh between an ostrich egg's weight and a hummingbird egg's weight.
How many children could share this chocolate egg?
Name things that could be carried in an Easter basket.
Draw a design that could be put on an Easter egg.

Hank Aaron broke the home run record in baseball.

Hank broke Babe Ruth's record of 714 home runs. In the days after he broke the record, he received over 900,000 letters. The U.S. Post Office thought this was a record amount of mail for one person to receive. Hank Aaron eventually scored 755 home runs in his lifetime. **How many more home runs did he score after he broke the record?**

Name other baseball players and the records they have broken.
How is a baseball like a hammer?

Design a stamp to honor Hank Aaron.
What baseball player will be the next person to have a stamp designed in his honor? Why?

The United States opens a free public library today.

Libraries became important with the invention of paper and the printing press. Harvard University's library, the earliest in the United States, was begun in 1638. Early libraries all charged their patrons a fee to borrow books. On April 9, 1833, a tax-supported library was opened in Petersborough, New Hampshire. People could now borrow books for free. The idea of the free library quickly spread to other towns. **If Jamestown, the first American colony, was settled in 1607, how many years later did the first library appear?**

How are books like adventures?
How is a library like a peanut butter and jelly sandwich?
Start a class list of all the library books that the students read each month.
Categorize the books and make a graph to show what kinds of books your class reads.
Design a bookmark to celebrate libraries.

From A Good Resource
April 1 - 9 Math Days
from Mathmagical Moments
by Sue Heckler & Dr. Christine Weber
Pieces of Learning, 1995

▲ Joe Wayman

Reading poetry is a delightful way for teachers and students to practice their questioning skills. It is especially fun when the poetry is from the book ***Don't Burn Down the Birthday Cake*** by Joe Wayman. The purpose of Joe's poetry is to help children explore and come to terms with their own feelings and to experience a more positive sense of self. The poem, "Teddy Bear" helps children realize they are not alone in their feelings; that all people experience the same hope, fear, pain and joy.

TEDDY BEAR

I first saw him sitting there,
A great big fat and furry bear.
Bright and shiny button nose,
Yellow zippers, boots and bows.
I knew at once he had to be,
A Teddy bear meant just for me.

I picked him up, he seemed to fit,
He snuggled 'neath my chin a bit.
That Teddy Bear came home with me,
And sometimes sits upon my knee.
I bump him sometimes on his head,
And thump him till he must be dead.

I snuggle him and huggle him.
He's always there through thick and thin.
My friend when I have messed up bad.
My friend when I am sad or glad.

When I fall and skin my knee.
He's always waiting there for me.
When I need a special friend,
He sits beside me till the end.

The world is filled with pain and care,
And when there's sorrow I must share,
I'll make it through 'cause he is there,
Teddy Bear, my Teddy Bear.

And when he's gone and lost his hair,
And when his fuzz is almost bare,
I'll love him then, yes, I'll still care,
Teddy Bear, my Teddy Bear.

From A Good Resource
Don't Burn Down the Birthday Cake
by Joe Wayman
Pieces of Learning
Beavercreek OH

▼ A FEW "BEARY" GOOD QUESTIONS

There are no right or wrong answers to these questions that refer to **TEDDY BEAR**. They are useful to stimulate thinking and self expression. Respect the child's opinions as they respond and you will develop a trust between you and the student.

If you have a teddy bear as a friend, what qualities does it have that real friends don't have?

What kinds of feelings do you share with your teddy bear?

Does your teddy bear always agree with your opinions?

Discuss the following statements . . .

There is no such thing as security.

It makes me feel secure to be home in my own bed.

It doesn't bother me when my parents take a vacation without me.

What is meant when we say someone has a security blanket?

Why do you think people need security blankets? Do you have one?

Compare/contrast a teddy bear with a real bear.

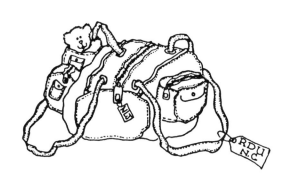

List all the uses for a teddy bear other than as a stuffed toy.

What kind of bear trap might catch a teddy bear?

Could you design a better teddy bear so more people would buy one?

What would happen if all adults in the world needed to carry a teddy bear around with them at all times?

 BOB STANISH

Questioning has found a real friend in Bob. His many idea books for teachers focus on divergent questions. Bob's mission in life seems to be to nurture creative thought in teachers and their students. His books offer creative ways to explore feeling as well as thinking, because the author's experience has convinced him that "knowledge grows more vigorously, and is employed most meaningfully, when combined with human sensitivity." The following questions from three of Bob's books are excellent examples of his insight and talent. They are published by *Good Apple*.

I Believe in Unicorns

List all the ways you can think of to get a hippopotamus out of a bathtub.

What would things say to each other in your mother's grocery bag . . . if they could talk?

If you could stir a rainbow, what kind of design would you give the sky?

List the goods and the bads about having an octopus serve as a lifeguard.

Sunflowering

Quick liners for a Thursday morning:

Which of your numbers would hurt the most if you were a dial telephone?

Which weighs more — a promise or a mistake?

If you could squeeze an additional hour into a 24-hour day, between which two hours would you squeeze the 25th?

If you were a human clock, at what time would you prefer your arms?

Mindglow

In what ways would life be different if there were no shadows?

In what ways would life be different if memories were only retained for a year?

List things easy to forget.

List things that can be reversed.

What would it be like to be a leaf that feeds the soil?

What would it be like to be a secondary rainbow?

You will not rush though a Bob Stanish book. You will travel slowly, allowing time for connections and extensions, time to believe in unicorns again, time to watch a sunflower flower, and time to experience a mindglow. Enjoy!

▼ QUESTIONING AS A LIFE SUPPORT SKILL

<u>There's Something About A Bridge . . .</u>

A few years ago, the great states of Kentucky and Illinois joined hands and pocketbooks across the mighty Ohio River to build a beautiful new bridge. The day of dedication was truly a time of celebration for all the folks of Paducah, Kentucky and Metropolis, Illinois who had braved the old narrow metal bridge for far too many years. Of course the long haul truckers were probably the most grateful. Over the years, an untold number of side mirrors had been sacrificed in head-to-head, side-to-side meetings in the middle of the bridge. The CB radios always had plenty of chatter about the perils of "the old tin can crossing the Ohio."

Yes, there's something about a bridge, new or old, that sparks conversation and a certain measure of imagination. However, as remarkable as the steel and concrete variety is, it's those "other bridges" - the ones that defy architectural explanation - that are the most difficult to build.

The other bridges in question are those involving the human spirit and its need for survival. They include the bridges between childhood and adulthood, between learning the basic skills of life and applying them, between emotional fulfillment and leisure time, and between human potential and success in life. The master builders of these very special bridges are TEACHERS.

When the aforementioned bridges are successfully combined, they form the LIFE SUPPORT SKILLS children need. Four of the most important life support skills are: dealing with frustration, breaking mind sets, asking different kinds of questions, and learning to work with others. In this book I have dealt with Questioning.

QUESTIONING

One of the greatest bridges in preparation for the squiggles in life is differentiated Questioning skills. Teachers must model as well as teach the process of balancing basic recall, right/wrong answer questions with divergent, no right/no wrong answer Questions. It is an important learning tool that stimulates high level thinking and strengthens self concept. The Questions children will face as adults will not always have right or wrong answers. Children need practice in asking as well as answering divergent Questions so they will feel confident using them as adults.

When practiced consistently, Questioning becomes an active, not passive, process that motivates teacher and student

POSTSCRIPT

My high school English teacher, Mrs. Kenward, must have said it at least fifty times! "Write about your own experiences, your own life. Write what you really know about—YOU!" So, here goes, Mrs. K.

Recently I experienced my version of "Questioning Makes the Difference." It started with a call from my tax accountant just two weeks before the dreaded April 15th showdown.

"I hope you are sitting down," she said. "I hope you made a major mistake in the totals you gave me," she said. "I hope you have a winning lottery ticket in your pocket," she said. Finally, SHE SAID, "It looks like you have underestimated your quarterly tax payments."

I immediately started guessing how much. "More than that," she said. I guessed again. "More than that," she said. I think after the third or fourth guess I stopped listening because my brain had gone numb.

In the few days that followed I robbed Peter to pay Paul until the funds could be collected. By April 15 my numbness had turned to anger. Of course, there wasn't a soul in sight to blame. The entire soap opera with the accompanying stress could have been avoided if I had only practiced what I had preached so many times to so many parents, students and teachers. ASK QUESTIONS! ASK MANY QUESTIONS! ASK MANY DIFFERENT QUESTIONS!

I share my real life experience with you to illustrate the importance of Questioning in our day-to-day existence as humans. This has been a book about Questions, not answers. It is based on a philosophy that Questions are more important than answers. In many classrooms, students are taught to answer, not to Question. Without realizing it, educators begin an unfortunate pattern that students carry with them into life and the real world. There are teachers who are trying to break that pattern. They desperately need the support and encouragement of administrators and parents.

The Questioning skills in this book are really LIFE SUPPORT SKILLS. Whether it's about careers, personal health, politics, education, the environment, the past, the present, the future, or even TAXES! there are Questions to be asked.

Bibliography

Aylesworth, Thomas G., and Gerald Reagan. *Teaching for Thinking.* Garden City, New York: Doubleday, 1969.

Balsamo, Kathy. *It's About Writing.* 1990. *Thematic Activities for Student Portfolios.* 1994. Beavercreek OH: Pieces of Learning, 1990.

Bellanca, James, Robin Fogarty, and Kay Opeka. *Patterns for Thinking.* Chicago, Illinois: Illinois Renewal Institute. 1985.

Bloom, Benjamin S., and David R. Krathwohl. *Taxonomy of Educational Objectives.* New York: David McKay Co., Inc. 1956.

Bruner, Jerome S. *A Study of Thinking.* New York: John Wiley, 1956.

DeBruin, Dr. Jerry. *Creative Hands-On Science Experiences.* Good Apple. 1980.

Eberle, Bob. *SCAMPER.* East Aurora, New York: D.O.K., 1971.

Eberle, Bob and Bob Stanish. *CPS for Kids.* East Aurora, New York: D.O.K., 1980.

Frank, Marjorie. *If You're Trying to Teach Kids How To Write You've Gotta Have This Book.* Nashville, Tennessee. Incentive Publications, 1979.

Gudeman, Janice. *Creative Encounters With Creative People.* Good Apple, 1985.

Heckler, Sue, and Dr. Christine Weber. *Mathmagical Moments.* Beavercreek OH: Pieces of Learning, 1995.

Johnson, Nancy L. *The Faces of Gifted.* 1989. *Parenting Skills for the 90s: Your Gifted Child.* VHS, 1989. *Teaching Skills for the 90s: Questioning Makes the Difference.* VHS, 1990. *Teaching Skills for the 90s: Strategies & Activities to Stimulate High-level Thinking.* VHS. *Parenting Skills for the 90s: The Parenting Puzzle Piece by Pieces.* 1991. *Thinking is the Key.* 1992. *The Best Teacher 'Stuff".* 1993. *Active Questioning.* 1995. *Look Closer* 1996. Beavercreek OH: Pieces of Learning.

Osborn, Alex F. *Applied Imagination: Principles and Procedures of Creative Problem Solving.* New York: Charles Scribner's Sons, 1963.

Parnes, Sidney. *Creativity: Unlocking Human Potential.* East Aurora York: D.O.K. Publishers, Inc. 1972.

Patterson, Claire. *Let's Celebrate Math.* Beavercreek OH. Pieces of Learning, 1990.

Pincus, Debbie. *Interactions.* Good Apple, 1988.

Polette, Nancy. *Books and Thinking Skills.* O'Fallon, Missouri: Book Lures: 1988.

Raths, Louis E. *Teaching for Thinking: Theory and Application.* Columbus, Ohio: Charles E. Merrill, 1967.

Raudsepp, Eugene. *More Creative Growth Games*. New York: Perigee Books, 1980.

Stanish, Bob. *I Believe in Unicorns*. 1979. *Mindglow*. 1986. *Sunflowering*. 1977.Good Apple.

Stock, Gregory. *The Book of Questions*. New York: Workman Publishing. 1987.

Szabos, Janice. *Reading-A Novel Approach*. Good Apple, 1984.

Von Oech, Roger. *A Whack On the Side of the Head*. New York: Warner Books, Inc. 1983.

Wayman, Joseph. *The Other Side of Reading*. 1980. *Secrets & Surprises,* 1977. Good Apple. *Don't Burn Down the Birthday Cake* (book and audio cassette).1988. *I Like Me* (Activity book and audio cassette) 1989. *If You Promise Not to Tell*. 1991. Beavercreek OH: Pieces of Learning.

Williams, Frank E. *Classroom Ideas for Encouraging Thinking and Feeling*. Buffalo, New York: D.O.K. Publishers, Inc., 1970.

The New Games Book. More New Games. San Francisco, California: The New Games Foundation. 1980.